DATE DUE

MAR 03 '05			

DOSTOYEVSK

With a little more ti
a work of which m
world continues to
The Idiot and *Crim*

Judith Gunn ex
contradictions

A noblema
distrusted for
hero. An outs
adult life in f
selling auth

A deeply
writings. Ju
consciousne
Orthodox w

Dostoyev
to rule with
have expect
than a social
beloved hon
what was an

JUDITH GUN
book, a biog
Having first
explore both
attempted t
story. It is t
Dostoyevsky

TO SIMON

DOSTOYEVSKY
Dreamer and Prophet

Judith Gunn

A LION PAPERBACK
Oxford · Batavia · Sydney

Copyright © 1990 Judith Gunn

Published by
Lion Publishing plc
Sandy Lane West, Oxford, England
ISBN 0 7459 1575 2
Lion Publishing Corporation
1705 Hubbard Avenue, Batavia, Illinois 60510, USA
ISBN 0 7459 1575 2
Albatross Books Pty Ltd
PO Box 320, Sutherland, NSW 2232, Australia
ISBN 0 7324 0259 X

First Edition 1990

British Library Cataloguing in Publication Data
Gunn, Judith
    Dostoyevsky : dreamer and prophet.
    1. Fiction in Russian. Dostoevski, F. M. (Fedor
    Mikhalovich), 1821-1881
    I. Gunn, Judith
    891.733
    ISBN 0-7459-1575-2

Library of Congress Cataloging in Publication Data
Gunn, Judith.
    Dostoyevsky : dreamer and prophet / Judith Gunn. — 1st ed.
    p.   cm. — (A Lion paperback)
    Includes bibliographical references.
    ISBN 0-7459-1575-2
    1. Dostoyevsky, Fyodor, 1821-1881—Biography.   2. Novelists,
    Russian—19th century—Biography.   I. Title.
    PG3328.G85   1990
    891.73'3—dc20
    [B]

Printed and bound in Great Britain
by Cox and Wyman Ltd., Reading

CONTENTS

1	The Poorhouse	7
2	The Cycle of Violence	15
3	The 'Furious Vissarion'	24
4	Arrest	32
5	The Shadow of the Executioner	39
6	Reprieve	48
7	The Wives at Tobolsk	52
8	The 'Unfortunates'	57
9	Freedom in Exile	65
10	Love and Marriage	73
11	The Tower of Babel	81
12	Underground Man	89
13	The Raising of Raskolnikov	98
14	The Gambler	110
15	Atheism and Sin	121
16	The Gadarene Swine	127
17	Debts and Credit	135
18	The Dream	142
19	The Brothers	154
20	The Prophet	163
	Bibliography	169
	Index	172

Do you know that I am absolutely aware
that if I could have spent two or three
years at that book — as Turgenev,
Gontscharov and Tolstoy can — I could
have produced a work of which men
would still be talking in a hundred years
from now.

FYODOR DOSTOYEVSKY, 1870

Chapter One
THE POORHOUSE

Moscow's Mariinsky Hospital for the Poor was a place of death for the poverty-stricken people of the city. Few left its premises cured. The diseases that afflicted them varied, but the most consistent killer of their time was tuberculosis. The rich could stave off such chronic illnesses with mountain air, rich food and a personal physician. But the patients at the Mariinsky could not afford such attention and so they depended on the ministrations of men such as Dr Mikhail Andreyevich Dostoyevsky.

Mikhail Dostoyevsky had begun his medical career as a military doctor. His father and grandfather were priests in the Uniate church, a 'denomination' in the Ukraine. The Uniates attempted to reconcile Catholicism and Orthodoxy by using the practices and rituals of the Russian Orthodox church while accepting the authority of the Pope. Despite this clerical background, however, Mikhail Dostoyevsky broke with the family tradition and at the age of twenty left home, without his father's blessing, to study medicine.

His Uniate background provided him with useful knowledge for his medical training. In order to be conversant with Roman Catholic liturgy he had learned Latin and so was able to grasp medical Latin with ease. After training at the Imperial Medical-Surgical Academy in Moscow he went into the army. His skills were first tested at the battle of Borodino, the last great conflict before Napoleon entered an evacuated Moscow only to be forced back along his own scorched route by the Russian Army, the Cossacks and 'General Winter'.

While Mikhail struggled to save just a few of the half-million or so lives lost in the campaign, his future wife, Maria Fyodorovna Nechayeva, was fleeing Moscow with her family. Those who escaped the city in 1812 had no time to organize their evacuation and her father, a merchant, had to leave his business behind, losing almost everything. When the family returned they faced a less affluent future, so it became essential that the daughters should marry young. Maria's older sister married a successful merchant, one Alexander Kumamin. This wealthy couple were to be an important influence on Maria's children long after her death. By 1820 Maria had found a partner in Dr Mikhail Dostoyevsky. When their first child, also Mikhail, was born, Dr Dostoyevsky applied for a transfer out of the military and was given work in government service at the Mariinsky Hospital. It was there that their second son, Fyodor, was born in 1821, just a year after Mikhail.

The family moved into a small flat in a neighbouring building belonging to the hospital. The hospital itself had been built on the grounds of a cemetery for outcasts. Nearby was a transit station for prisoners being sent to Siberia, and Muscovites dubbed the whole area the 'poorhouse'.

The grounds of the Mariinsky Hospital were not the playground that most parents would have wished for their children, and the terminally ill and the chronically poor did not make easygoing, energetic companions. What concerned Maria Fyodorovna Dostoyevsky was not the poverty which forced the patients to come to the Mariinsky Hospital, nor their character, nor even the way they looked, but rather the illnesses that afflicted them. To be placed in such close proximity to diseases such as tuberculosis seemed a potent threat to young lives.

Maria and her husband told their children not to speak with the patients, but their second son, Fyodor, did not always abide by their rules. Despite warnings from his father and threats that he would one day end up in prison himself, he and his older brother often led their younger brothers and sisters on illicit adventures in the hospital's grounds. Sometimes they would stop and talk with the lonely figures who walked in the fresh air within the limited confines of the hospital.

Fyodor lived for most of his childhood at the hospital. Here he first observed the consequences of poverty on human lives, and against this background he came to understand the link between poverty and ill health. He saw that often those who could not pay could not get the treatment they needed. He came to realize that, for many, poverty meant death. His early experience left him unafraid of the 'poor' as people, although justifiably afraid of poverty itself. It gave him an insight into the harsher side of life which, as an adult, he was not afraid to portray. His first published novel, *Poor Folk*, was about people like the ones whose faces filled his childhood.

In Russia at that time the law stated that only the nobility could own land or property with serfs. The Dostoyevsky family had once been noble, but some of their Orthodox ancestors were stripped of their titles when they refused to convert to Catholicism. Because the family was no longer noble, Dr Dostoyevsky had little say in the choice of his family's accommodation, but like many of his stature he did employ servants — there were seven in the small apartment at Mariinsky Hospital. Even so the family Dostoyevsky could never compete with Aunt Kumamina who occasionally visited the apartment in a carriage drawn by four horses and equipped with a footman and postilion. Her arrival was not always welcomed by Fyodor who, like his father, came to regard the Kumamin's show of wealth as vulgar.

Home life for the Dostoyevsky children was regimented but not cruel. Silence had to be maintained between the hours of two and four in the afternoon when Dr Dostoyevsky took a siesta. In the summer, the children were required to sit by their father while he rested and keep the flies from disturbing his rest. In the evenings Dr Dostoyevsky would read aloud to the family. Both parents instilled in the children a love of stories, art and literature. Dostoyevsky was greatly affected by his first trip to the theatre to see *The Robbers* by Schiller. No doubt he was also grateful for the evenings when both parents went out and their mother instructed Alyona, their nurse, to let the children have some play time.

Dr Dostoyevsky believed in the value of discipline and education. In addition to his work at the hospital and his own private practice, he took the time to tutor his children, teaching them Latin and insisting that they learn French. He saw education as the key to their advancement in a world fraught with class differences, and he was not a lenient teacher. The boys had to stand to strict attention in Latin classes while repeating Latin declensions. Dr Dostoyevsky was quick to lose his temper if a mistake was made which, in Fyodor's case, was quite often. Dr Dostoyevsky did not believe in corporal punishment and consequently he never hit his children. The worst punishment that he felt he could inflict on the boys when they failed to meet his standards was to walk out on them during a lesson. To deny them education was the ultimate punishment. This was quite progressive thinking for a man of his time.

Although Dr Dostoyevsky studied medicine, not theology, he did not desert his father's faith. The family ended each day with prayers said before the icon, and they employed a deacon to teach the children Scripture. He was a gifted man who retold Bible stories with fire and colour, bringing the familiar tales to life. Maria, too, was well acquainted with the traditions of Orthodoxy, for her grandfather had been a proof-reader at the Ecclesiastical Press in Moscow. She taught Fyodor to read using a text of retold stories of the Old and New Testaments. Of his early childhood Dostoyevsky said, 'We in our family have known the Gospel almost ever since earliest childhood.'[1]

Their nurse, Alyona Frolovna, told the children stories of ancient Russia, of Saint Sergey of Moscow subduing a bear by the power of his holiness, of heroes and legends and folk tales, Christianity and Russian myth intertwined. Her stories were so vivid that sometimes she held the children transfixed and some nights they went to bed too afraid to sleep.

Christianity did not reach Russia until AD988, when Kiev became the first Russian Christian city. In successive centuries Moscow survived both the attacks of Genghis Khan and his Mongol Empire and the more persistent threat from Islam and the Turkish Ottoman Empire. Allied with the East against Rome, after failed negotiations and theological disputes, Moscow became the only independent representative of Orthodoxy (most other Orthodox nations were under the heel of the Turkish Empire). As a result, Orthodoxy flourished in Muscovite Russia.

The form of Christianity that entered Russia from the Byzantine Empire remained rooted in the Eastern and Greek traditions of spectacular churches, gorgeous icons and an unchanging liturgy. The beauty of Orthodox buildings and the magnificence of their icons owed much to their wish to capture something of heaven on earth. In their churches the artists tried to portray what God's holy kingdom would be like. In their icons they tried to present the saints in their heavenly form. Icons were not intended to be idols. They were not to be worshipped, but were to help the worshipper visualize the perfect state and so meditate on it and pray to God through that state of mind.

The Dostoyevsky family were devout and once a year they visited the Trinity Monastery of St Sergey, the patron saint of Moscow, to pray and fast and retreat from the hospital. The monastery, sixty miles from Moscow, was a centre for healing, possessing an ornate and gilded reliquary, and was a popular place of pilgrimage.

At least once a year the young Fyodor could gaze upon the richness of a church built in the Orthodox tradition of Byzantium. He could take part, from the earliest age, in the rituals of the Eucharist, for the Orthodox church allow much more participation by children in the sacrament from the moment of baptism than do most Protestants and Roman Catholics. He could repeat a liturgy which had remained almost unchanged for nearly two thousand years. He could watch the long-haired, bearded priests leading the congregation in worship amid a wonderland of gold, colour and candles. But this glimpse of magnificence was a rare event for the Dostoyevsky family. The monastery was a contrast to the 'poorhouse' district in which they lived. The golden domes of the Kremlin that flashed in the sunlight were different indeed from the cold stone of the hospital, and the richly costumed priests were a change from the drab and ragged patients in the hospital grounds. It is not surprising then that the adult Dostoyevsky was to concern himself with the paradox of human suffering permitted by a loving and awesome God. Even as a child he was greatly moved and fascinated by the biblical story of Job, who lost everything he had because God gave the devil permission to test him to the limit.

Despite his occasionally serious preoccupations with stories such as Job, however, Fyodor was still a small boy and his main concerns were not theology. His father tried to make him read

11

an introduction to Orthodoxy by Metropolitan Filaret of Moscow, a contemporary theologian, but analytical theology was neither the Orthodox church's strength nor Fyodor's.

Mikhail and Fyodor shared a room. Two more brothers and three sisters were to survive to share their home, but Fyodor remained close to Mikhail throughout his life. Among their childhood friends, outside the family, was one girl who was to end her life tragically. Only nine years old, she was found dying in the hospital grounds after being raped. The manner of her death was to have a profound effect on the growing Fyodor. It was for him the first indication of the real evil of humankind. In his later novels Dostoyevsky was uncompromising in his portrayal of similar crimes and their effect on both victim and perpetrator.

In 1828, when Fyodor was seven, his father was promoted and regained for the family their noble status. This did not catapult them into the ranks of the aristocracy. There was a vast difference between nobles in service and the more exalted noble class, but they did receive certain privileges and could now own land. Three years later, anxious about the hospital as a place for children to grow up, Dr Dostoyevsky bought a small acreage with 'seventy-six souls'. 'Souls' were defined as the male serfs who worked the land. The term did not include their families.

The land and smallholding were in a place called Darovoye, approximately a hundred miles from Moscow. Financially it was not a wise purchase and Dr Dostoyevsky was financially crippled by a second purchase he made to ward off an unfriendly neighbour. Not only that, the Dostoyevskys knew nothing about farming or land owning, the soil was poor and the house itself was little more than a run-down cottage. None of this, of course, bothered Fyodor and Mikhail. Their parents were right to think it would do the children good to get away from the oppressive buildings of the Moscow hospital, and they revelled in Darovoye.

The children spent their summers playing Robinson Crusoe and cowboys and Indians. Fyodor was the leader in the games and chose for himself the best roles. He preferred to be Robinson and the cowboys. The children had space and sun and a whole new way of life to explore. Their pranks were energetic and usually harmless, but on one occasion they stole the icon from the local chapel and paraded it round a field in an imitation church procession. This was considered by all adults concerned to be going too far.

At Darovoye, for the first time, they came into prolonged contact with rural peasants. Serfdom was no easy way to live, but for the children Darovoye was a country haven.

All new places hold their terrors for children and the vast spaces of the open countryside and flourishing forests were no exception. One day Fyodor had been playing quietly in the woods, probably looking for a suitable stick to hit frogs with, as he recalled many years later[2]), when he heard someone shout, 'Wolf! Wolf!' Wolves had not been seen in that area for several years, but the shout was so clear and so urgent that Fyodor wasted no time in running to the open fields. There he found a peasant, Marey, working with a plough. Marey, somewhat bemused by the little boy's terror, had heard nothing, but he calmed the boy down and assured him that there were no wolves. He told Fyodor that he must have been dreaming, and instructed him to cross himself for protection. Only partly convinced, Fyodor dusted himself down, crossed himself and began to walk back to the house. The peasant promised that he would watch until the boy was safe. When Fyodor looked back, the peasant was still watching him.

Whether the wolf and the warning cry ever existed can never be proved. But on that day in Darovoye Dostoyevsky heard a voice. It may have been the product of an over-active imagination or an indication of the epilepsy he was later to develop. Such incidents in his life have been attributed to aural hallucination. In his novels, Dostoyevsky would portray various kinds of hallucinatory experiences, using illusion as well as ordinary dreams as literary devices.

Poor harvests, run-down facilities and ignorance were enough to make the estate go under, but Darovoye suffered another, more serious blow. Early in 1833 the estate was destroyed by fire. Maria had taken charge of the land while her husband worked in the hospital. Now all her attempts to put the business on a successful footing lay in ashes. The family was devastated. They had had such high hopes of their rural home, and the serfs in their care were now homeless and without food. The outlook was so bleak that the

Dostoyevsky's nurse, Alyona, offered the family all her savings to help pay their debts. The family did not accept her offer, but years later Fyodor would remember the generosity of a poor woman who offered all that she had to her employers.

The summers at Darovoye came to an end. The fire and the birth of her last and seventh surviving child had weakened Maria considerably. For some years she had been fighting tuberculosis. On 27 February 1837 she called her family into her bedroom, blessed them all, prayed once more before the icon and died. Fyodor, now fifteen, mourned her deeply.

Hers was not the only death to grieve him that year. He had inherited his mother's love for literature and had come to adore the poetry of Aleksander Sergeevich Pushkin. Unfortunately Pushkin burned brightly and died young, killed in a duel. According to his brother Andrei, when Dostoyevsky received the news of Pushkin's death, he would have asked — if they had not already been in mourning for their mother — permission to go into mourning for Pushkin.

Literature had become Fyodor's first love, but his father did not regard literature as a safe career. Mikhail and Fyodor, who had both planned for a university place and a life with literature, were smartly informed that they were to apply for entrance to the Military Academy for Engineers. With that decision, or so young Fyodor believed, their future was ruined.

Prelims quotation: Letter to Sofia Alexandrovna, August 1870, *The Letters of Fyodor Michailovich Dostoyevsky to His Family and Friends*, page 205.

[1] 'One of the Contemporary Falsehoods', *Diary of a Writer*, page 152.

[2] 'Peasant Marei', *Diary of a Writer*, pages 205–10.

Chapter Two
THE CYCLE OF VIOLENCE

'With the cry of "now", the mare tugged with all her might, but far from galloping could scarcely move forward; she struggled with her legs, gasping and shrinking from the blows of the three whips which were showered upon her like hail. The laughter in the cart and in the crowd was redoubled, but Mikolka flew into a rage and furiously thrashed the mare, as though he supposed she really could gallop.'[1]

Dostoyevsky told the story of the cruel death of the mare in the first of his most famous novels, *Crime and Punishment*, but it was almost thirty years earlier that he had witnessed the scene that would influence his work so directly in the years ahead.

Mikhail, Fyodor and their father were on their way to St Petersburg. It was the spring of 1837. There had been no persuading their father that a military career would not suit them. Dr Dostoyevsky had made up his mind. After his wife's death he had grown increasingly anxious about his children's future. He was not a rich man; nor could he call upon the advantages of an 'old boy network' or aristocratic privileges to find them places in the civil service or finance their university education. He and Maria might have instilled a love of literature in their two sons, but literature would not provide them with a living. In a world where only status could unlock the doors to wealth and success, a military career would allow them to rise through the ranks and achieve respect and job security.

The two teenage brothers viewed their future with apprehension. They had not anticipated a career in the army. They had never dreamed that they would study mathematics and engineering, and they did not look forward to parade ground drill, military exercises or the possibility of military action. Even so, they could not resist the excitement of leaving home. The promise of independence and the thought of St Petersburg set them dreaming optimistically of adventures and kept their minds off the prospect of hard military discipline.

The journey to St Petersburg took a week. En route they met fellow travellers, observed something of Russian peasant life and counted the days before their arrival in St Petersburg, when they could exchange their uncomfortable carriage for solid ground. Among their fellow travellers on the road were businessmen and merchants, other journeying families, the occasional soldier and government messengers.

One evening the Dostoyevsky party stopped at an inn for something to eat. From their table they could see a postal station where couriers exchanged their exhausted horses for fresh and speedy ones. While they watched, a government courier dashed into the station, probably for a glass of vodka, and then returned to his new horse and cart to continue his journey. Hardly had the man settled in his seat when he began punching his driver in the neck with all his power and shouting at him to get a move on. Again and again his fist crashed down on the driver's neck, and in the same rhythm and with the same persistence the driver's crashed down on the horse's back.

Dostoyevsky was horrified, not so much by the display of unprovoked cruelty as by the way in which it was perpetuated from the courier to the driver and from the driver to the horse. Years later, in his journal, *Diary of a Writer*, he recalled the scene and the effect it had on him. 'This little scene appeared to me, so to speak, as an emblem, as something which very graphically demonstrated the link between cause and effect. Here every blow dealt at the criminal leaped out of each blow at the man.'[2] He imagined the driver's shame and the mockery he would receive at home because of his bruised neck. He imagined his rage at being so publicly punished, and he perceived that the cycle of violence might not have stopped there but may have extended to the man's wife and children in an attempt to expiate the violence perpetrated on him. In a Russia where, for a few, power over another human being

16

was easy to come by, this may have seemed an ordinary event, but for Dostoyevsky it was a graphic, unforgettable, illustration of the injustices of serfdom.

Soon, however, his brooding was interrupted by their arrival in St Petersburg — Russia's 'window on Europe'. In St Petersburg the moneyed classes lived with grace and ease, influenced by European trends. There was a growing feeling among many of Russia's wealthy that Western Europe was to be courted and imitated. Those who had the time and the money indulged themselves in what Europe had to offer — art, fashion, even scientific knowledge. Not that it was safe to espouse every Western idea: Tsar Nicholas I employed strict censors to make sure that no ideas that could threaten his political position were permitted to spread either in public discourse or in print. Those who lived in St Petersburg had to be particularly careful as they lived within sight of the Tsar.

The Tsar's reactionary policies may have had something to do with the unsteady beginnings of his reign. In December 1825 he hesitated before accepting the throne after his brother's death, for he had not prepared himself to be the Tsar. While he was making up his mind, a small group of officers, known as the 'Decembrists', rebelled and raised a mutiny against him within sight of the palace. He then felt obliged to take the throne for the sake of stability. The officers refused to stand down and there was some bloodshed before the revolt was routed and the Decembrists punished by execution, prison or exile. Nicholas, then, was haunted by the brief but potent spectre of revolution in his own palace, and the people of St Petersburg took care not to offend him. This was the climate the Dostoyevsky brothers first encountered in St Petersburg. The apparent liberality of the literary circles was, to some extent, an illusion and the fate of the Decembrists was a more realistic measure of the level of the freedoms Dostoyevsky could expect.

All that was of little relevance, however, to the young Dostoyevsky, who would grow to love St Petersburg with its picturesque streets and canals and its apparent atmosphere of free discussion. Moreover he and Mikhail were to be together, or so they thought, free from their father's stern regime.

17

This at least would compensate for having to join the army cadets.

Their first destination in the city was not the military academy in which their father hoped to enter them but a preparatory school for the necessary entrance exams. Throughout the summer the brothers studied hard, so that by the autumn they were ready for the examinations. When they arrived to take the exams, however, they discovered that entrance was gained by bribing the officials rather than by academic achievement. Mikhail failed to gain entry on the grounds of ill health, and Fyodor was refused a scholarship. The boys had not realized that they should offer bribes to the examiners and, even if they had been warned, they did not have the money with which to make such offers.

Dostoyevsky felt the injustice of this keenly. He wrote to his father: 'I heard recently that after the Examinations, the general used his influence for the acceptance of four of the new entrants at government expense, as well as for the candidate from Kostomarov's who robbed me of my vacancy. — What meanness! I was thunderstruck! We, who have to struggle for every rouble, have to pay, while others, rich men's sons, are taken free, damn them!'[3]

It looked for a while as if Dr Dostoyevsky's plan to enter his sons in one of the best military schools in Russia would fail, but Aunt Kumamina came to the rescue and paid Fyodor's fees. She and her husband were childless and throughout their lives took a keen, if patronizing, interest in Maria Dostoyevsky's children. Fyodor himself was never really grateful for their generosity and tended to resent them more for what they did not give than be thankful for what they did.

The brothers were separated: Fyodor entered the St Petersburg school and Mikhail was sent to a less fashionable academy at Reval, five hundred miles away.

For the next six years Dostoyevsky was to study engineering in a building that had once been a palace — something of a contrast to the Mariinsky Hospital in Moscow. Fyodor had done well to gain any kind of place at the academy, but his time there proved to be a mixed blessing. From the beginning he felt at a social disadvantage. Most of the officers in training came from a higher and richer class of nobleman than he did, and he felt pressured to imitate their life-style. He wrote frequent letters to his father requesting money which he spent enthusiastically. He needed new galoshes, he pleaded, and a new cap for the parade so that the Tsar would not notice him in the old one. It is difficult to see how the Tsar could have noticed one cap in a sea of thousands of men on parade, but Dostoyevsky felt that he must keep up appearances.

In addition, he was developing his lifelong addiction to tea and he needed money for tea to keep him warm after exercises: 'When one has to sleep in a canvas tent during damp and rain, or when, in such weather, one returns weary and chilled from practice, one may easily fall ill for want of tea, as I have frequently experienced in former years at these times.'[4] Dr Dostoyevsky always struggled to find the money he requested, for he was determined that his son should have the best start in life that he could provide.

His father's regime may have been strict but it played its part in preparing Dostoyevsky for taps and reveille and strictly disciplined lessons. The work at the academy that most suited him was the training to be a draughtsman — though his designs were sometimes more inventive than practical. He once designed a fortress that had no doors, presumably because that seemed to him the most logical way of ensuring that it would be impenetrable. His design did not amuse his superiors, including the Tsar. He never lost his interest in architecture: his later notebooks contain sketches that are evidence of his talent.

Fyodor did not get on well with some of his instructors and, when he was failed in one year's exams and forced to repeat that year, he claimed that he had been victimized by his tutors. Dostoyevsky's letters to his brother at that time are full of self-righteous indignation and the claim that his marks were clearly good enough to allow him to progress on to the next year. He conveniently forgot to mention his less good results.

His contemporaries at the academy remembered him as a pale and withdrawn youth, always reading, in a uniform that never seemed to fit. When he was officer of the watch he took a book with him and studied at night, a habit he never lost. He pored over the works of Victor Hugo, Walter Scott, Pushkin and George Sand. Maths was not his strength, but he showed an active interest in religion lectures, often staying behind to talk to the tutor, a priest. For his faithful observance of Orthodox practices he earned himself the nickname 'Monk Photius'. Perhaps his religious studies and observances helped him keep his sense of identity as a spiritual being and an artist in a military world with which he did not identify, full of uniformity, engineering and mathematics.

He was often seen reading the Bible and the works of a German-Swiss writer and novelist, Zschokke, who believed that Christian love should have a social application resulting in social justice. In his own situation Dostoyevsky was not slow to defend the newer and younger lads against the usual boys' school cruelty and bullying. As a consequence, his friendships within the academy were limited and, although not friendless, he remained something of an outsider.

One friend, however, made Dostoyevsky's time at the academy more bearable and introduced him more intimately to the world of literature and art. Shidlovsky did not live in the academy but worked in the finance department of the huge Russian civil service. The two men shared a love of literature and, perhaps, the fact that neither of them was doing what he really wanted. Although only five years older than Dostoyevsky, Shidlovsky's experience was enough to guide Fyodor through his first two years in St Petersburg and to provide him with a mentor. Together they studied literature, and Shidlovsky probably encouraged Dostoyevsky to write.

Shidlovsky was an exciting influence on his friend, but he was hardly a stable character. His moods shifted from ecstatic faith in God to overwhelming despair and doubt. He embodied much of what Dostoyevsky would explore in his work: the inability of the rational mind to understand the mysteries of God. The main character in one of Dostoyevsky's earliest novels, *The Double*, probably draws on Shidlovsky's wild swings between faith and despair.

During those early years Shidlovsky was Dostoyevsky's most favoured companion, more so than his brother. 'Knowing Shidlovsky has given me many hours of a higher life, but that was not the reason. You perhaps criticized me, and will criticize me again, for not writing to you; my stupid military circumstances were the reason for that. But I must tell you the truth, my dear:

I was never indifferent to you, I loved you for your poems, the poetry of your life, and your unhappiness — and that was all; the love of a brother, the love of a friend, I did not feel for you.'[5]

The friendship was not to last, however, for although Dostoyevsky never lost his affection for his friend, Shidlovsky went into a steady decline and they lost touch. He was reputed to have a great talent as an orator, but a brief spell in a monastery ended in disgrace when it was discovered that Shidlovsky had caused some other monks to turn to alcohol. It was drink that contributed to his death in 1872.

In June 1839 the message came that Dr Mikhail Dostoyevsky was dead. After Maria's death he had given up his job at the hospital and moved back to Darovoye, now decimated by fire and famine. The doctor did not recover easily from his grief. When he was not wandering the house in search of Maria he was either drinking himself into a stupor or taking comfort in the arms of a peasant girl on the estate. His treatment of his serfs was at best petulant, at worst cruel.

There were no witnesses to Dr Dostoyevsky's death. His son Andrei stated that he was murdered during an angry row with his serfs. Some said that he was ambushed, dragged from a carriage and suffocated with a cushion, others that in a fit of temper he provoked the peasants into an attack; others that he had drink poured down his throat and was then suffocated; yet others that he was severely mutilated. Not everyone thought it was murder: some said that he had an apoplectic fit. All the evidence anyone had to go on was that Alyona heard a scream.

Medical investigators found no evidence of violence, despite repeated accusations by the neighbour with whom the Dostoyevskys had argued since their purchase of Darovoye. The body was left where it fell for two days, but although this was regarded by some as suspicious, by others it was seen merely as the strict application of local law to ensure that the authorities saw the body where it fell. Bringing charges was also a fraught business: no evidence could be found that the serfs actually did it other than hearsay. But if the serfs had committed the crime they would have been sent man, woman and child to Siberia, thus rendering the land valueless. Without serfs to work the land it could not be productive, and so land at that time was valued as much by its workforce as by the area it covered or its fertility. The spreading of a murder rumour could therefore have been advantageous to the neighbour who had long had his eye on Darovoye and could pick up the land cheap if the serfs were convicted and banished to Siberia. This could have given the Dostoyevsky family a motive not to 'investigate' the crime themselves, however. Whatever the truth, the authorities did not prosecute the serfs; this in itself is an indication that Dr Dostoyevsky probably died from natural causes, for the government was keen to clamp down on attacks on landowners.

Whether Dostoyevsky believed his father was murdered is doubtful. Unless the evidence of the medical enquiries and hearings never reached him, which is unlikely, he would have known that medical opinion concluded that Dr Dostoyevsky died of natural causes, and even if he had doubts, the theory of murder was not the only possibility. Dr Dostoyevsky's daughter Lyubov certainly believed that her father was murdered, and the psychologist Sigmund Freud also accepted the murder theory, suggesting that it accounted for Dostoyevsky's pre-occupation with parricide in his last novel, *The Brothers Karamazov*. However, his interest in parricide may have more to do with the characters he met while he was in a Siberian prison than with the death of his own father. In Siberia, crimes of all sorts were revealed to Dostoyevsky, giving him plenty of material to work into his fiction. Whatever the cause, Fyodor Dostoyevsky was now orphaned and his younger brothers and sisters went to live with the childless Kumamins, a fate of which Dostoyevsky did not approve but could do little about, as he too was in their debt.

He did not see his father's sudden death as an opportunity to escape the academy. Despite the fact that it did not suit him, it was a safe path. It allowed him to stay in St Petersburg; it provided him with accommodation and, later, a job. His independence was now not only assured, but inevitable, and he could leave the military when he was ready. A lifetime in the army did not necessarily stretch before him. For now he concentrated on keeping his head above water at the academy and teaching himself all he could about literature.

He read voraciously, often at night, and he attempted to translate the French novel, *Eugénie Grandet*, by Balzac. He also began to write: soon he would make his first serious and successful attempt at writing a novel.

[1] *Crime and Punishment,* page 58.

[2] 'Russian Society for Protection of Animals . . . ', *Diary of a Writer,* page 186.

[3] Letter to Dr Dostoyevsky, February 1838, *Dostoyevsky: A Self Portrait,* page 8.

[4] Letter to Dr Dostoyevsky, May 1838, *The Letters of Fyodor Michailovitch Dostoyevsky to His Family and Friends,* page 2.

[5] Letter to Mikhail, January 1840, *Dostoyevsky: A Self Portrait,* page 14.

Chapter Three
THE 'FURIOUS VISSARION'

In 1841 Dostoyevsky passed his exams. In 1842 he was promoted to second lieutenant and in 1843 he moved outside the academy, assuring himself of more time to pursue his own interests, especially writing and reading.

In the next few years he moved several times, always trying to get an apartment near a church. Perhaps this was an attempt to keep in touch with the earthly evidence of his beliefs. Though he could not know it, his faith was about to meet its first major challenges.

His first move, near St Petersburg's Vladimir cathedral, was to an apartment he shared with Adolph Totlebon, a man from high society whose brother, Eduard, would soon become a Crimean War hero. Such a flatmate probably pleased Dostoyevsky's sense of society, especially when, later in life, he found he needed all the well-placed friends he had. Not many of his flatmates found him easy to live with, however, and he had a high turnover of companions.

One Dr Riesenkampf shared his rooms for a while at the recommendation of Mikhail, who felt that the doctor might have a stabilizing influence on his brother. Mikhail, like most of Dostoyevsky's relatives, was alarmed at the speed with which Fyodor could lose money. Already he had begun to gamble in a small way, usually losing at billiards. He was not a careful guard of his money, either. On at least one occasion his cash was stolen and, when it was not stolen, he was inclined to give it away. Dr Riesenkampf ran a surgery for down-and-outs from the flat and often Dostoyevsky would spend his last roubles on the men who told him their tragic life stories. Riesenkampf felt that these characters reappeared in Dostoyevsky's powerful descriptions of poverty, drink and illness. Their wasted lives provided original material for the young writer.

When money ran out, Dostoyevsky borrowed from Riesenkampf or sent heart-rending letters to his brothers begging for money. He fought hard to get an advance on his inheritance, sending insistent, sometimes petulant, letters to the Kumamins who were trustees of the estate. They capitulated finally and sent him five hundred roubles despite the fact that this would create hardship for the rest of the family. He lost it within twenty-four hours.

Dr Riesenkampf noted Dostoyevsky's frequent mood swings. When he was with people he was animated and jolly. He communicated his love of literature with such passionate speeches that his friends were held spellbound until well into the small hours. But once alone in the flat he would shut the door on the world and remain in his room, often deeply depressed.

Dostoyevsky was not an easy sleeper either; he frequently complained to Riesenkampf that he was prevented from sleeping by the sound of someone else in the room, snoring. He did not in fact share his room with anyone and this may be another example of the kind of aural hallucination that Dostoyevsky experienced as a child when he heard the cry of 'wolf' in the forest. Dr Riesenkampf later attributed Dostoyevsky's moods and eccentricities to the workings of a great mind wrestling with the sufferings of humanity and preparing to convey it to the world in his writing. In spite of this charitable evaluation, however, Dr Riesenkampf moved out of the flat before Dostoyevsky began writing his first novel.

Although Dostoyevsky had been in no hurry to leave the military academy when his father died, he did not expect the military to become his life's vocation. He used it to earn money. However, in 1844 he discovered that this secure living was about to make serious inroads into his chosen career. Having learned that he might be sent a good distance away from St Petersburg on an inspection mission, he applied to be released from the military on the grounds of ill health. In October 1844 he was struck off the lists of the Corps of Military Engineers. Now his writing was his only occupation, and so it became vital to get his work published.

Dostoyevsky thus locked himself in his room for many hours at a time, furiously writing what would be his first novel, *Poor Folk*. His new flatmate was Dmitry Grigorovich, a fellow writer who turned out to have influential friends.

Dostoyevsky said later that the novel just dropped into his mind when he was walking on the banks of the River Neva in St Petersburg. It was a bitter cold evening, his breath cracked in the air and the river itself was frozen. As the sun set it flamed the mist over the river, and in the swirling clouds he saw another city take shape. Living in this new city, in sadness and poverty, were his two protagonists: Dievushkin, a middle-aged civil servant, and Barbara, a penniless young woman. They wrote letters to each other, tracking the progress of their lives until the end of their doomed romance. Dostoyevsky went home and started writing.

In the following months he wrote and rewrote the story, some of it during his summer stay with his brother at Reval. Back in St Petersburg, he sent his newly married brother a commentary on how it was going, but he did not reveal anything to the ever-curious Grigorovich until he was sure that the much revised manuscript was ready for its first reading.

One summer day he emerged from his room, having painstakingly copied out a neat version, and told his friend to sit down and listen. Within a page or two Grigorovich realized he was listening to a brilliant work. He interrupted Dostoyevsky to tell him so, but Dostoyevsky was too anxious to respond easily to his friend's enthusiasm. He insisted that Dmitry just sit down and listen without interrupting. Grigorovich did as he was told, and as he listened his conviction grew that here was a genius.

Grigorovich was acquainted with a young man of literary talent and entrepreneurial abilities and he wasted no time in getting the manuscript to this man, Nikolai Nekrasov, for his opinion. They were going to read only a few pages at first, so that Nekrasov could get an idea of what it was like, but after ten pages they read another ten, and then ten more, until they finished the whole novel in the small hours of the morning. At the last scene, where the lovers are forced to part, Grigorovich could no longer control himself and started to sob. When he looked up, he saw that Nekrasov too was weeping. At the end of the reading the two could hardly bear to look at each other, for tears were streaming down both their faces.

At four in the morning they returned to Dostoyevsky's flat to wake him up and tell him the great news that they loved the novel, and Nekrasov wanted to publish it. They would take it to Vissarion Belinsky, Russia's most influential literary critic of the time. They left Dostoyevsky pacing up and down his room, unable to sleep, nervously anticipating Belinsky's reaction.

Recalling the scene later, Grigorovich admitted that it was probably a bit impetuous to wake Dostoyevsky so suddenly and give him the good news. 'I must confess that I had acted rashly. For I knew the character of my housemate, his morbid sensibility and reserve, his shyness — and I ought to have told him all quite quietly next morning instead of waking him in the middle of the night, and, moreover, bringing a strange man to visit him!'[1]

Dostoyevsky had read and admired Belinsky's work for several years now and all he could think of, after his visitors had gone, was that soon the great man would be reading what he himself had written. When some weeks later, it was time for Dostoyevsky to meet Belinsky, Nekrasov had to work hard to persuade Dostoyevsky to come. Even though by then Dostoyevsky knew that Belinsky also thought *Poor Folk* was a work of genius, he still could not see why the great critic would want to meet him.

Belinsky, or the 'Furious Vissarion' as his friends called him because of his passionate oratory, was the son of a navy doctor and the grandson of a priest. One of a new breed of Russians known as the 'plebeian intelligentsia', he was not of aristocratic birth, so had to earn his living. He did this, not through the traditional channels of priesthood, medicine or the civil service, but through his education: he was a freelance journalist. Although catapulted into journalism by being expelled from university in 1832, he soon became an influential literary critic and socialist thinker. Believing that literature should serve the aims of social justice, he received *Poor Folk* enthusiastically and gave it his support.

Dostoyevsky's first novel is the story of two lovers trapped by their poverty into making declarations of love that have little hope of fulfilment. Like a documentary, it describes in authentic detail the everyday living conditions of the poor. Its stark realism highlights the injustice of their situation and cannot fail to move the reader. Although an unashamedly sentimental tale in which Barbara eventually marries another, richer man, it was very different from the fashionable literature of the 1830s, which imitated German and Italian romanticism.

Belinsky believed he had found the new genius of Russian literature, and Dostoyevsky soon came to agree. 'I go to see Belinsky very often. He is incredibly well-disposed towards me, and in all seriousness sees in me a demonstration to the public and a vindication of his opinions.'[2] So wrote Dostoyevsky to Mikhail in 1845, but he was not quite the perfect demonstration of Belinsky's opinions that both of them at that time believed.

Both men were attracted to the ideas of the French writer Fourier who stated that because all current economic structures were riddled with injustice, only a complete destruction of these structures would result in any kind of social justice. The people were to be persuaded to live in 'phalansteries' of about eighteen hundred persons in a single building which contained auditoriums, lecture theatres, dance halls and the like. In these phalansteries social justice would be practised and a new, almost physical law would inevitably result, as tangible as Newton's theory of gravity. It was the law of social harmony. According to Fourier, then, the barrier to social harmony was social injustice, not human nature. There is no doubt that Russia in the nineteenth century was not a just society. In the eighteenth century serfs had made up 45 per cent of the Russian population. They lived more or less without rights. Their owners could sell them without land, split up families, tell them who to marry and punish them.

Dostoyevsky, keenly aware of the injustice inherent in the Russian feudal system, was attracted by the Fourier solution. Through reading Zschokke he had come to believe in social justice as a Christian imperative; and Fourier's philosophy, although radical, spoke of economic, not political, reform. It did not seem to threaten the political structures of the Russian nation; phalansteries could be built without tearing down the existing system of government.

But Belinsky's beliefs went beyond Fourierism. He was also influenced by the rationalist philosopher Hegel and by the theologian Feuerbach, whose book *The Essence of Christianity* suggests that all religion is the projection of humanity's wish to believe in God. By the time Belinsky and Dostoyevsky met, Belinsky had not only renounced Christ but had come to regard religion as harmful. In Russia, the Orthodox tradition had taught a passive faith for centuries.

It seemed to many Russian socialists that the Orthodox church complied with a cruel and autocratic regime in oppressing the peasants. It offered colourful rituals and religious awe, but no solution to the serf's poverty. Reward, it taught, would come in heaven. It was this view of religion that led Marx to proclaim it the 'opium' of the people. Belinsky had come to believe that religion was not even that. The people, he said, rejected religion. They used it as a superstition and held few priests in high esteem. It was harmful and divisive and was better destroyed. In order to be a true socialist one must be an atheist: God had no place in the phalanstery.

Dostoyevsky later wrote of Belinsky: 'Still as a socialist, he had to destroy Christianity in the first place. He knew that the revolution must necessarily begin with atheism. He had to dethrone religion . . . [3] The Furious Vissarion argued his case cogently. He believed that if Christ had been born in Imperial Russia he would have been effaced by the evil of the regime. Dostoyevsky did not go quite so far. As Belinsky spoke, he caught sight of Dostoyevsky. 'I am even touched to look at him,' he said. 'Every time I mention Christ his face changes expression, as if he were ready to start weeping.'[4] Dostoyevsky argued that if Christ had been born in their time, he would at least have joined the left. This Belinsky conceded, unwillingly.

Belinsky represented the first philosophical challenge to Dostoyevsky's faith and Christian practice, and many aspects of his new peer group's ideas attracted him. His contemporary work and letters, however, suggest that he did not give up his faith entirely.

Religious differences were not the main cause of Dostoyevsky's sudden fall from grace in the Belinsky circle. Arrogance was the more likely reason: Dostoyevsky was carried away by the praise of his peers, and he did not endear himself to his new-found friends. He lorded it over other, more junior, writers, or he reacted jealously to the attention they were getting. An intense relationship with the renowned writer Ivan Turgenev, which had the potential to become a lifelong friendship, turned sour almost as soon as it began. Their differences were so great that, over thirty years later, Dostoyevsky and Turgenev had to be chaperoned at gatherings for fear of a row between them. Dostoyevsky wrote to his brother that he was almost 'intoxicated' with his own fame.[5] Not only did Dostoyevsky antagonize the group; his much awaited second novel *Golyadkin*, or *The Double*, disappointed Belinsky and Nekrasov. The novel, a fantasy about a man who discovers that his evil double is taking over his life, was the first representation of a theme that was to dominate Dostoyevsky's thinking as he grew older: the question of how one individual can be the source of both great evil and great good.

According to the realistic humanist Belinsky, the novel was not a relevant social document but an exercise in fantasy and psychology. Art, Belinsky maintained, exists to serve the higher needs of public justice. In a utopia, art would serve the state. By contrast, fantasy and psychological analysis serve no real purpose in the material world and therefore are not appropriate. Art that is not socially useful is not art. Moreover, the utopian socialist denied one of the foundations of the novel: that a human being could have an evil side as well as a good one.

Dostoyevsky soon found himself in a minority of one. Belinsky and Nekrasov began to think they had misjudged his genius and they were not kind in their retractions. Dmitry Grigorovich, perhaps not all that tactfully, reported all the gossip to Dostoyevsky. With *The Double*, Belinsky said, this genius had hit bottom. A cartoon portrayed Dostoyevsky as a red pimple on the nose of literature. The last straw came when, at one of their gatherings, Turgenev took the opportunity to mock him through a caricature of a provincial man who dreamed he was a genius. No names were mentioned, but Dostoyevsky got the point and left the group, never to join the Belinsky circle again.

[1] Reminiscences of Dmitry Grigorovich, 1837 to 1846, *The Letters of Fyodor Michailovitch Dostoyevsky to His Family and Friends*, page 267.

[2] Letter to Mikhail, October 1845, *Dostoyevsky: A Self Portrait*, page 32.

[3] 'Old People' *Diary of a Writer*, pages 6–7.

[4] *Ibid.*, page 7.

[5] Letter to Mikhail, November 1845, *Dostoyevsky: A Self Portrait*, page 34.

Chapter Four
ARREST

The St Petersburg social life of the 1840s was dominated by literary cliques which were essential to the success of its writers, and now Dostoyevsky was no longer a part of one. Although he was ostracized from the Belinsky circle, his relationship with Belinsky himself continued amicably for some time. Even that relationship, however, was to end in an exchange of sharp words early in 1847. Once again Dostoyevsky found himself out in the cold.

The year after their final argument Belinsky died. The news hit Dostoyevsky hard. Death had denied him the opportunity for further debate with Belinsky and had denied them both the chance for reconciliation.

The night he heard of Belinsky's death he stayed at the home of his friend and doctor, Stepan Yanovsky. During the night Dostoyevsky suffered some form of convulsions, possibly an early indication of the epilepsy that was not to be officially diagnosed until nearly a decade later.

Intellectual debate continued among Belinsky's followers, but never with the same heat that the 'Furious Vissarion' had brought to the discussions. Moreover, times were changing and many, including Dostoyevsky, were soon to pay a high price for holding and expressing radical views.

Despite setbacks, Dostoyevsky was still a well-known author and not, as yet, a revolutionary. His main concern was his work and its reputation. His first novel had been an unqualified success and, although his second book had a mixed reception, some critics defended it. These allies soon sought Dostoyevsky out and invited him to join another literary clique.

Valerian Maikov not only liked Dostoyevsky's second novel, *The Double*; he defended it publicly in his own review. He replaced Belinsky as chief literary critic of the journal *Notes of the Fatherland*, published by Krayevsky who had also published Dostoyevsky's second novel. Before his death Belinsky had left *Notes of the Fatherland* to join a magazine revived by Nekrasov and called *The Contemporary*. This division in publications was a tangible representation of the division in opinion and friendships that was to last throughout Dostoyevsky's life, with only limited reconciliation in later years. This was partly because Dostoyevsky himself could not make the move to *The Contemporary*, as some of his colleagues did. Being short of money, he had bound himself to the publisher Krayevsky and owed him work for *Notes of the Fatherland* in return for the advances he had already spent.

Krayevsky was a shrewd businessman and not open to negotiation on the subject of money. He went on to ruin a friend of Dostoyevsky's whom he exploited so badly after buying him out of twenty-five years of national service that the young man died in poverty and despair. However, the contacts and friends Dostoyevsky made through *Notes of the Fatherland* brought him into a literary clique known as the Beketov circle. This circle centred mainly on the Maikov brothers, Valerian and Apollon.

Necessity may have brought Dostoyevsky into contact with the Beketov circle, but he now began to make lifelong friendships. The views expressed by the members of the circle, like Dostoyevsky's, took much more account of Christianity than had the atheistic socialism of the Belinsky group. Theirs was a Christian socialist utopia. Christ and Christianity demonstrated socialist principles as they were meant to be. Christianity put a moral imperative on the Christian to act justly and to work to improve the lot of the poor. Jesus Christ became both a model for ethical behaviour and a rebuttal of Fourierism: the teaching that moral corruption results from an unjust environment. Jesus, born in an occupied country, suffered the ultimate injustice and yet did not turn into a murderer or a criminal. He was not shaped by what had happened to him but maintained moral integrity in spite of his environment.

This may have been a humanist approach to Christ's teachings and example, but these ideas were congenial to the Dostoyevsky who had looked offended when Belinsky had condemned Christ and religion. Had the Beketov literary circle lasted longer, Valerian Maikov's leadership and the propagation of his ideas might well have stabilized Dostoyevsky's own vacillating Christian opinions.

The Beketev group, however, disintegrated a short time after Dostoyevsky joined them. On this occasion it was not because of philosophical differences but the result of a tragedy: Valerian Maikov died in a drowning accident aggravated by sunstroke. Once again Dostoyevsky found himself without a clique, and his ideas were fluid enough at that time to be moulded by the strength of the characters he met rather than his own strength of mind. His next group of friends was to be a dangerous mix of strong-minded radicals.

Mikhail Petrashevsky was an outrageous man, even by today's standards. He was reputed to have turned up at an Orthodox mass dressed as a woman. He owned a large library, mostly of banned books, which he lent out. He was one of the authors of a clever book called *A Pocket Dictionary of Foreign Words* which used the pretext of defining new words to communicate radical ideas without incurring the wrath of the censors. Dostoyevsky met Petrashevsky while he was walking one evening in Nevsky Prospect, in St Petersburg. A young man who had been talking with a mutual friend approached him and asked what the idea for his next story was.[1] The man was Petrashevsky, and Dostoyevsky soon found himself with new friends — Petrashevsky's literary and political circle which met on Friday nights.

In terms of the development of Dostoyevsky's Christian thought, this was a step backward. Like Belinsky, Petrashevsky advocated the ideas of Fourier, David Strauss and Feuerbach. Strauss had written a life of Christ that investigated the role of myth-making in the story, and Feuerbach had stated that all religion was, in effect, man's wishful thinking. Petrashevsky had a low opinion of Jesus' capabilities and referred to him as a demagogue who came to an unhappy end.

Religion was not the only matter for debate. Petrashevsky, like Belinsky, believed in the inherent good in human beings; evil, he thought, was caused by an unjust environment. He believed that, should he start chatting with a murderer on a railway-station platform while waiting for a train, a transformation would take place. As the two men described each other's life stories, Petrashevsky would be able to convince the murderer that his crime was a product of his oppression. The conversation would end in tears, the two men on equal terms: one repentant for his crime because he was forced, by circumstances, to do something against his nature and the other glad to have freed that murderer of his responsibility, having taken some of it himself. Both men would now be able to anticipate an ideal life in a better world.

The Petrashevsky circle discussed passionately the injustices committed against the serfs and the need for reform. Some of the group, however, were dissatisfied with mere discussion and were looking for more direct action. A few thought it was time to stop talking and do something about injustice.

Dostoyevsky's articulate defence of the serfs attracted the attention of Nikolai Speshnev, recently returned from five years in Europe studying communism, revolutionary politics and, especially, the effectiveness of secret societies as a revolutionary tool.

In the Petrashevsky circle Speshnev found some supporters for his ideas on direct action and Dostoyevsky was one of them — particularly after Speshnev shrewdly lent him five hundred roubles. Speshnev, Dostoyevsky and others joined the Durov circle, a circle within a circle, a secret society with specific aims and goals, a secret oath and a call to arms come the revolution.

Secret societies always pose a threat to an autocratic regime. A strong enough oath of allegiance to a group and of opposition to the government could be incriminating in itself, and could allow the society to get a grip on its members. Speshnev had become an expert in this kind of manipulation. The paranoid Tsar Nicholas I opposed all secret societies, especially when violent revolution erupted in Europe in 1848. In March of that year there were uprisings in Vienna, Berlin, Venice and Milan. Soon France and Rumania heaved to the rhythm of revolution and self-government. The barricades and call to arms Speshnev had planned for in Russia became a reality in France and in Austria, where a temporary government in Vienna declared itself in favour of Hungarian independence. The Tsar was not complacent. Hungary, on the borders of Russia, for a short time expressed some very radical views. It seemed to Tsar Nicholas that Russia was the only stable government in Europe, and he intended to keep it that way. He set up a committee to monitor all publications and to apply strict censorship. Schools and universities were seen as breeding grounds of subversion, and it became increasingly difficult to publish anything but the most reactionary works in support of Russia and the Tsar. An informer was placed in the Petrashevsky circle and began watching what went on there.

Dostoyevsky always asserted that he did not support violent revolution and that he did not conspire to assassinate the Tsar. No doubt this proved true, for the informer could find no evidence to the contrary. Neither could he be sure of the existence of the secret society, nor name any possible members of that society. But the open activities of the Petrashevsky circle were incriminating enough. Dostoyevsky was asking for trouble because he openly opposed censorship. Strict censorship, he said, meant that the people could never be educated about new ideas, that there could never be a popular movement for change because the people would not know how their situation could be changed. Dostoyevsky and his companions planned to attack censorship head-on: they would purchase a printing press so that they could spread ideas among the general public and let the people do the rest.

One night Apollon Maikov received a visit from Dostoyevsky, who explained their aims and said that they needed money for the printing press. Maikov was horrified. He warned Dostoyevsky that this could lead to serious trouble. What kind of revolutionaries, he asked, would poets and artists make? Dostoyevsky begged Maikov to join the group but he refused, although he promised to say nothing about it.

Dostoyevsky was not unaware of the seriousness of his situation and his health began to deteriorate. His doctor and friend Stepan Yanovsky noted that he saw Dostoyevsky often during his association with Speshnev and treated him for nerves, hypochondria, dizziness and hallucinations. Some of these symptoms may have been the precursors of his epilepsy.

Opinions vary as to when the seizures started. His old flatmate

Grigorovich stated that Dostoyevsky had a convulsion when they came across a funeral procession in St Petersburg. Perhaps this was a result of the sight of the trappings of death. Sigmund Freud suggested that his epilepsy was brought on by his father's death, although it is unlikely to have been evident as early as that, or it would have ended his career at the military academy. Yanovsky noted that Dostoyevsky's best guard against these attacks was prayer, and even though Dostoyevsky got increasingly involved with the Durov circle he still did not neglect his religious duties. Whatever the source of his problem, as the conspiracy became more and more demanding, Dostoyevsky was increasingly plagued by ill health.

At one of his consultations with Yanovsky he said that he had a 'Mephistopheles' of his own. He mentioned no names but Speshnev seemed the most likely candidate for such a role. Speshnev had succeeded in grabbing his loyalty, in spite of his better judgment. Once again Dostoyevsky was trapped by debt and perhaps his own impetuosity, for now that he was implicated as a secret society member he could not leave the group.

Dostoyevsky seemed well aware that the Petrashevsky circle's days were numbered, although he did not know there was an informer in their midst. He nevertheless continued to involve himself in the circle's activities. On 7 April 1849 the circle met beneath a portrait of Fourier to celebrate the philosopher's birthday. Dividing up his book and distributing it among themselves in segments, for translation, they were now most definitely indulging in the propagation of subversive ideas.

Dostoyevsky went still further. At three meetings he publicly read and apparently endorsed a letter from Belinsky to Gogol which proclaimed ideas that were anathema in the Russia of Tsar Nicholas.

Nikolai Vasilievich Gogol, the influential author of such works as *The Inspector General*, had in 1847 written a treatise praising the Russian peasant people, lauding Orthodoxy and supporting the current autocratic regime. Belinsky responded to Gogol in a letter stating that religion was harmful, that the peasants hated it and that they held the clergy in little esteem. Belinsky saw the Orthodox tradition as a yoke under which the peasants suffered.

If they expressed any religious thought at all, he said, it was mere superstition. By condemning Orthodoxy Belinsky attacked the very root of Russian social structures and the authority of the Tsar over his people. This was the letter Dostoyevsky recited aloud three times in public.

The informer, Pyotr Antonelli, reported this to his masters, and they showed the Tsar the evidence he had gathered. The order went out to smash the Petrashevsky circle. At four in the morning of 23 April 1849, just after Dostoyevsky had gone to bed, he was disturbed by somebody in his room. As he woke up, he heard the sound of military boots and the rattle of a sabre in its holster. He was addressed by his military rank, 'Engineer Lieutenant Dostoyevsky', and informed that he was under arrest. As he dressed hurriedly, all his books and belongings were pulled down from their shelves and his letters and writings were sealed with wax to prevent tampering. By the end of the following day he was in solitary confinement in a cell in the St Peter and Paul Fortress, a prison reserved for only the most dangerous prisoners.

[1] *Dostoevsky as Reformer: The Petrashevsky Case*, page 46.

Chapter Five
THE SHADOW OF
THE EXECUTIONER

'Take a soldier and put him in front of a cannon in battle and fire at him and he will still hope, but read the same soldier his death sentence *for certain*, and he will go mad or burst out crying. Who says that human nature is capable of bearing this without madness? Why this cruel, hideous, unnecessary, and useless mockery? Possibly there are men who have sentences of death read out to them and have been given time to go through this torture, and have then been told, You can go now, you've been reprieved. Such men could perhaps tell us. It was of agony like this and of such horror that Christ spoke. No, you can't treat a man like that!'[1]

The walls of Alekseyevsky Ravelin in the St Peter and Paul Fortress were thick, damp and lined with mould. The ravelin, the strongest fortification in the prison, had housed and seen murdered the son of Peter the Great. It had watched the bodies of those too weak or too long incarcerated to last their stay taken out of the fort by night to be ferried down the river to their graves. It had presided over the doom of the rebel officers who had challenged Tsar Nicholas I when he first came to the throne. It was soon to open its doors to Dostoyevsky and his friends.

The prisoners of the Petrashevsky circle were each placed in solitary confinement with only rats for company and very little light, except that which came from a high-up and heavily barred window. Because the cells were always dim, the prisoners had to burn candles continuously so that the eyes behind the long narrow slit in the door could see what they were doing. At the start of their imprisonment they were allowed no letters, no books, nothing to write with and no tea. For all they knew they had been buried alive and left to rot, not only imprisoned but forgotten. Their rebellion, little more than a conspiracy, had been thwarted before they could attract attention to their cause. There had been no heroic acts by which the people could remember them; they hoped there would be no martyrs.

In July, when conditions were eased and Dostoyevsky was allowed to receive and write letters, he wrote to his brother Mikhail, 'If I am not allowed to write I shall perish. Better fifteen years in prison with a pen in my hands!'[2] While enduring that very deprivation, however, he had continued to use his imagination, planning novels in his head. Once allowed pen and paper he wrote a short story, 'A Little Hero', first published anonymously in 1857, while he was still in Siberia.

Solitary confinement, poor food, lack of information and little stimulation took their toll on the prisoners. When they finally saw each other again, almost eight months later, they were thin and unshaven, some very ill and others worn down by loneliness and fear.

Despite the fact that Dostoyevsky entered prison already run down, suffering from nervous exhaustion and perhaps showing some symptoms of epilepsy, his health did not deteriorate as drastically under the prison regime as might have been expected. He was surprised at how well he coped with the prison routine and squalid conditions. He wrote to Mikhail: 'Meanwhile I am still alive and well, for all that . . . I expected much worse, but now I see that there is such a store of vitality inside me that it cannot be exhausted.'[3]

Perhaps imprisonment even came as something of a relief to him. His doctor, Stepan Yanovsky, had already observed how nervous and tense he was just before his arrest and had diagnosed several of his problems as hypochondria. Apollon Maikov had noted that Dostoyevsky was very agitated when he arrived on his doorstep that night to try to persuade him to join the secret society and contribute to the printing press enterprise, and Dostoyevsky himself had referred obliquely to Speshnev as his 'Mephistopheles'. All this may indicate that Dostoyevsky, well aware of the seriousness of the situation, found the tension and guilt affecting his health.

Apollon Maikov had painstakingly explained to him the dangers of his activities and, though Dostoyevsky did not take his advice, he could not have failed to understand it. He must have been aware that such a venture could only be doomed. Now that the worst had happened, the uncertainty was over. He had only to live through the consequences of his actions. He was in prison and would probably be sent to Siberia, but that would be the end of it. He need no longer speculate as to the severity of his punishment or when judgment day might be. It had already come, or so he thought.

Even if his nervous disposition improved, Dostoyevsky still faced physical threats to his health in the Alekseyevsky Ravelin. The water always tasted foul and so, not surprisingly, stomach problems were a constant complaint for most prisoners. At one time Dostoyevsky suspected that he suffered from scrofula, a form of glandular tuberculosis. Despite the unhealthy conditions in the prison, however, Dostoyevsky told his brother, 'There has never yet been working in me such a healthy abundance of spiritual life as now.'[4]

Fyodor was not the only Dostoyevsky arrested that night in April. His younger brother Andrei was also arrested and imprisoned, even though he had nothing to do with the Petrashevsky circle and very little to do with his brother's activities. Mikhail, their oldest brother, was on the fringes of the group through Fyodor. He had attended some of the meetings and shared some of Fyodor's views and aspirations. It was therefore probably Mikhail that the authorities were after, but they arrested Andrei because just before the raids he had briefly met with Fyodor in the street. The group was under surveillance by then and an identification of Andrei as Fyodor's brother may have been enough to condemn him.

Andrei spent only a short time in gaol and consequently was accused, by some, of pointing the finger at Mikhail, who was arrested a short time later. Fyodor did not believe those rumours: 'I remember, my dear, I remember when we met (I think it was the last time we met) in the famous White Hall. Then you would only to have had to say one word to the right person and you would have been freed at once, as having been taken by mistake in place of your elder brother. But you listened to my representations and entreaties; you great-heartedly comprehended that our brother was in straitened circumstances, that his wife had just had a child and not yet recovered — you grasped all this and remained in prison, to give your brother an opportunity to prepare his wife and as far as possible provide for her during what might be a long absence.'[5]

Fortunately, Mikhail did not spend much time in gaol either. He was released when the inquiry concluded that there was not enough evidence to link him with a deep involvement in the conspiracy. Fyodor, however, was a different matter.

Dostoyevsky's defence was a masterpiece of articulation. He did his best not to incriminate himself but was even more successful in not incriminating anyone else. When his questioners tried to force him to admit that the group held radical views on subjects such as serfdom, censorship or the church, he replied that there was usually so much arguing over these issues that he was at a loss to identify any united view that the Petrashevsky circle might have held.

The existence of the secret society centring on the Durov circle was never discovered. The bulk of the evidence against Dostoyevsky related to the fact that he had read Belinsky's letter to Gogol three times in public and that he had planned to set up a printing press. As far as the Tsar was concerned, the letter was a revolutionary document — a slander on Orthodoxy, the Russian people and therefore on the Tsar himself. Dostoyevsky defended himself on the grounds that simply reading out the letter was no indication that he sympathized with its views. 'Let him (the informer) recall whether there was in my judgements (from which I refrained) — or even in the intonation of my voice, or in my posture during the reading — anything that could in any way demonstrate my partiality to one party in the correspondence over the other?'[6]

When asked whether he agreed with Belinsky's letter, Dostoyevsky said that he did not agree with the 'exaggerations' in it. In this way he neither incriminated himself nor betrayed his real view of the infamous letter to Gogol.

His split with Belinsky was also a useful tool for his defence.

It was, after all, public knowledge that he and Belinsky had become enemies. Besides, he pointed out, in order to understand Belinsky's letter some reference had to be made to Gogol's views in the work to which the letter was a reply. Dostoyevsky had disseminated that information with as much eagerness as he had Belinsky's letter. This evidence, he suggested, could indicate that he agreed with Gogol and not Belinsky.

Dostoyevsky answered his questions alone before a court of six senior officials. All the others were interrogated in the same way. There is no evidence that these sessions of questions were brutal. Dostoyevsky suffered no significant hardship except that which separation and denial of liberty imposed on him. Apollon Maikov, who was taken in for questioning, remembered laughing with his interrogators as he tried to sketch out for them the architecture of a 'phalanstery'.

Petrashevsky, however, claimed to have been treated quite differently. According to rumour apparently originating with Petrashevsky himself, the Tsar was so incensed by the man's impertinent attitude that he himself got involved with the interrogation. The Tsar reportedly had electrical wiring connected between his palace and Petrashevsky's cell, so that he could inflict electric shocks on the man from the comfort of his home. It was also rumoured that the Tsar personally took Petrashevsky a poisoned drink which the prisoner refused; suspicious of the liquid, he stuck his fingers in it and was burned. There is little evidence for these stories. They were repeated by someone who met Petrashevsky on the road to Siberia and who claimed to have seen the burns on his fingers. Years later Dostoyevsky was to say that Petrashevsky was not in his right mind. He may indeed have told the stories, but it is as likely that he was suffering paranoid delusions as that actual torture occurred.

Officially the Tsar was not an interrogator. Among those charged with prosecuting the case, opinion varied as to the seriousness of the conspiracy. One senator, Lebedov, called them the 'child conspirators'; but the man in charge of surveillance, Liprandi, felt that their conspiracy posed a far greater threat to Imperial Russia than that of a student rebellion. Liprandi may have picked up some hints of the existence of the secret society centred on the

Durov circle, and he may have perceived a potential for subversion that went far beyond the plan to buy a printing press. With no hard proof he sensed more danger than that contained in a small discussion group.

By now Dostoyevsky's conditions had improved. Besides tea, new linen and writing utensils he was allowed some reading matter and so wrote to his brother asking for a Bible and the works of St Dmitry Rostovsky, Metropolitan of Rostov in the seventeenth century. Rostovsky was a story-teller, not a theologian; his stories of saints and martyrs perhaps reminded Dostoyevsky of his old Scripture teacher who had brought Bible stories to life. Now alone, without the pressure of his peers who attacked Christianity and sometimes mocked Christ, Dostoyevsky began to rediscover some of the old Bible stories and the teachings of Christ.

It is hard to determine just what went through his mind at this time, but it is possible that he began to recommit himself to the Christian faith during his prison years. He stated in a diary written and published in the 1870s that, at the time of meeting Belinsky, he had 'passionately embraced his teaching'.[7] From this evidence of his own later opinions it would seem that prison was a turning-point for his Christian beliefs. His later writings, however, tend to dramatize and simplify autobiographical material. By 1870 he interpreted his pre-prison beliefs as a sell-out to atheistic socialism and his post-prison beliefs as a commitment to Christianity. It was probably not as simple as that, for there is evidence to support the idea that he did have a commitment to Christianity, even during his turbulent youth. He and Belinsky disagreed on the subject of Christ and even in all the excitement of making new friends and testing new ideas Dostoyevsky never abandoned his childhood practices of attending religious services and observing fast days.

His time in prison gave him the opportunity to sit and weigh the various influences and ideas in his life so far. Alone and unhampered by the pressure of other people's opinions he could thoughtfully approach the question of faith and independently form his own convictions. His faith in God, whether continuing or revived, was growing stronger.

He was not struck with a beam of light in his cell, nor did he meet Christ at the door. The idea of sudden conversion was alien to the average Russian Christian of the time. Russia was largely untouched by the Reformation which re-emphasized the more personal and individual aspects of salvation. In nineteenth-century Russia an individual was born and baptized into the tradition of Orthodox Christianity, and therefore considered to be 'saved' as a child. The first initiation of a child into the Christian faith through baptism also brought them into full communion with the Christian community of the church: the sacraments of baptism, communion and confirmation being usually regarded as one rite. Orthodox church attendance was expected and often legally required.

Dostoyevsky therefore had the option to reject the tradition or to continue in it, but he had no need to be converted to it. Conversion was for the 'ignorant savage' in the 'heathen lands' and not for the sophisticated man born into the Christian tradition of Russia. Thus Dostoyevsky's relationship with organized religion was a lifelong tension between acceptance or rejection of the tradition into which he was born. Later he would embrace Russian Christianity as a force for mission in the world, but in the Alekseyevsky Ravelin he was just beginning to rethink his attitudes to traditional Christianity, and was still a long way from reaching any conclusions.

Dostoyevsky was tried before a military court, which demanded much harsher penalties than would a civilian court. On the conspirators, including Dostoyevsky, it passed sentence of death. An appeal for clemency was made on behalf of the prisoners, who were sentenced in their absence, and the Tsar acceded to this request, but not without one final act of cruelty that was to cost one man his sanity.

The Tsar secretly commuted the sentences of all the prisoners to varying lengths of imprisonment in Siberia, but he insisted that the death sentence should look as though it were to be carried out.

On the morning of 22 December 1849 the prisoners of the Petrashevsky circle were roused from their beds and ordered to dress. All they had to wear were the clothes they had worn in April when they were arrested: light spring clothes were not suited to the heavy snow and subzero temperatures outside. They were placed in covered carriages and driven to Semyonovsky Square. When they were let out of the carriages they saw each other for the first time in eight months. Some of their number were so changed that they were almost unrecognizable; others seemed undaunted by the months in prison. They greeted each other and turned towards the square. There, in the centre of a waiting crowd, was a scaffold hung with black cloth. Nearby were three stakes placed in the ground and a firing squad. It began to dawn on the conspirators just what lay in store.

'Do they really mean to kill us?' Dostoyevsky asked Durov, and the question circulated silently among them.

It seemed unbelievable when their only offence was talk, but the evidence of their own eyes was clear enough. In the cold and gloom, in their spring clothes, they listened to the death sentence being pronounced over them and they went through the rituals of the condemned. Swords were broken over their heads. A priest called them to repent and confess, but none was willing to renounce his beliefs and confess guilt. However, though they would not confess, they did all bend to kiss the cross. Dostoyevsky first watched and then went forward himself. Later he said that he felt he had understood nothing until he witnessed how his companions could not bring themselves to trifle with the cross. Its great significance and the enormity of what was about to happen to them kindled in them a last hope of faith.

'Today, December 22, we were driven to Semyonovsky Square. There the death-sentence was read out to all of us, we were given a Cross to kiss, swords were broken over our heads and our last toilet was made (white shirts). Then three of us were placed by the posts for the execution of the sentence. I was the sixth in order, we were called out in threes, consequently I was in the second batch and had not more than a minute to live.'[8]

It was a long and excruciating minute. The first three were led to the stakes and Petrashevsky, who was among them, yelled to his colleague to pick up his feet from the snow or else he would go to heaven with a cold. Soldiers tied them to the stakes and pulled the hoods of the shrouds down over their faces. Petrashevsky, however, managed to shake his free: he would see the last seconds of the dawn and the face of the man behind the gun.

The firing squad took aim and stood ready to fire. The minute stretched out, elongated until it was ready to split and still no one gave the order to fire. The men at the stakes shook with cold and fear. Dostoyevsky turned to Speshnev and said that they would soon be with Christ. Speshnev replied, that it was all 'a handful of dust'.

The seconds stretched into a second minute. Suddenly the prisoners heard galloping hooves and Adjutant General Sumarokov rode into view. From his horse, with a resounding stutter, he stammered out the commutation of the death sentence on all the prisoners. Instead of death, their destiny would be Siberia, at least for the next few years. The prisoners were stunned. The crowd was silent for a moment with shock, perhaps even disappointment, while at the stake Nikolay Grigoryev went mad.

[1] *The Idiot*, pages 47–48.

[2] Letter to Mikhail, December 1849, *Dostoevsky: Letters and Reminiscences*, page 9.

[3] Letter to Mikhail, September 1849, *Dostoevsky: A Self Portrait*, page 54.

[4] Letter to Mikhail, December 1849, *Dostoevsky: Letters and Reminiscences*, page 8.

[5] Letter to Andrei, June 1862, *Dostoevsky: A Self Portrait*, page 109.

[6] *Dostoevsky as Reformer: The Petrashevsky Case*, page 36.

[7] 'Old People', *Diary of a Writer*, page 9.

[8] Letter to Mikhail, December 1849, *Dostoevsky: A Self Portrait*, page 56.

Chapter Six
REPRIEVE

On that cold clear morning just before Christmas, the sun suddenly shone brighter for Dostoyevsky. Having faced death, he had never felt more alive. Even the sight of the ten-pound chains that he must soon wear could not dampen his new-found hope. He had been resurrected, allowed a second chance, and the air tasted sweeter and the prospects looked better than ever before. Life, not prison, exile or punishment was all that was important to him now; the rest was of little consequence beside the fact that he had escaped death.

Now the real sentences were read to the prisoners. Dostoyevsky's punishment was to be four years hard labour in a Siberian prison followed by four years as a private in Russia's army and an indefinite exile in Siberia. During this time he was forbidden to write or publish anything. His sentence would begin in two days.

The more dangerous Petrashevsky, by contrast, was allowed no goodbyes to any but those in the square. He was to be exiled immediately to do forced labour in the mines. He and the others were taken to another part of the podium where, as a prelude to their own futures, Petrashevsky's chains were hammered on. As the blacksmiths struggled with the chains Petrashevsky snatched a mallet from their hands and beat down on his chains, fixing them securely to his ankles. It was the act of a defiant man, determined not to let the authorities grind him down. Hypertense, but under control, Petrashevsky staggered clumsily to each of his comrades, hugging them and wishing them farewell. He then turned and stumbled towards the waiting cart. Before mounting he turned to look once more at his friends, drinking them in as they did him, and then bowed with a flourish, entered the cart and was driven off.

Back in his cell Dostoyevsky paced up and down, singing. The room was too small to contain his excitement. He was alive! What could so easily have been taken from him had been given back, and with it came a new responsibility.

'Now, as my life changes, I am born again in a new mould. I swear to you, brother, that I will not lose hope and that I will keep my body and mind pure! I shall be born again to better things. This is my one hope, my one consolation!'[1] Thus Fyodor wrote to Mikhail while he was waiting for his sentence to begin. Throughout his life he had feared death; in fact, many of his early convulsions had been associated with images of death. Now he had got close enough to death to taste it and had been given back his life. He was ready to grasp the new start and hold on to it.

Dostoyevsky was reminded of the work of another novelist, Victor Hugo, in his book *The Last Day of a Condemned Man*. Dostoyevsky had come to understand the condemned man's feeling that all that mattered was that he could see the sun. Nothing else was important: not material gain, not achievement, not fame. Dostoyevsky's brush with death could have made him terrified to move lest he bring the wrath of the authorities down on his head again. It did not. In fact it made him bold enough to face and survive Siberia.

He applied to see Mikhail one more time before leaving for Siberia. He had no idea what awaited him, whether he would be able to write letters, or read, or ever be released from his exile in Asian Russia. He wanted to see Mikhail for one last time. He hoped that they might one day meet again but at least, if they did not, their farewells would have been said. Permission was refused and for a while the exhilaration of reprieve was dampened by the prospect of separation during the bleak years ahead.

However Mikhail too had been asking to see his brother, and with more success. On the evening of 24 December Mikhail and a friend, Milyukov, gained entry to the prison to see two prisoners, Dostoyevsky and Durov, to wish them well on their journey and exile. The prisoners were brought into the room where Milyukov and Mikhail waited. Durov had suffered more severely from the prison regime. He was gaunt and ill whereas Dostoyevsky, although drawn and hungry, was still healthy.

The Dostoyevsky brothers hugged one another and Fyodor began to reassure the uncertain Mikhail that all would be well. They would see each other again, he said; he was confident he would survive his time in Siberia. Fyodor joked to Mikhail that his prison sentence was a good way to do research: it would give him plenty of copy for future books. Mikhail was not so optimistic.

Milyukov remembered the scene clearly: 'When the Dostoyevsky brothers took leave of one another, it was clear to me that not he who had to go to Siberia, but he who remained in St Petersburg, suffered the more. The elder brother wept, his lips trembled, while Fyodor seemed calm and even consoled him.'[2]

The visit was over all too soon, and now the Dostoyevsky brothers would be separated for nearly a decade. Dostoyevsky would not hear from his brother once during his four years in prison, a source of deep frustration and hurt to him. When he was released from prison, his first letter to Mikhail was as full of reproaches for not answering his letters as of doubts as to whether those letters or their replies ever got through. 'For God's sake, tell me why you have not to this day written a single word to me. Could I have expected this? Would you believe that in my solitary position, imprisoned as I was, I several times fell into actual despair, thinking that you were not even on this earth, and then spent whole nights brooding over what would happen to your children and cursing fate because I could be of no use to them?'[3]

Once the visitors had gone the two prisoners were taken to have their chains fixed to their feet. Those ten-pound chains were to be a permanent addition to their bodies for the full extent of their gaol sentences. They were given winter clothes to protect them on their journey and led to separate open sledges, so that they could pose no threat to their guards.

In the cold of the St Petersburg night the temperature was well below freezing. They were driven through the snow-solid streets of St Petersburg at dead of night. The streets were deserted, for the city itself was in a joyful mood. Christmas celebrations and parties were in full swing. The city did not brood about the fate of its 'unfortunates', as the prisoners of Siberia came to be known in Asian Russia. There was hardly a soul to see them start their journey. The people were inside in the warm, settling down for the feast. The sledges passed by the heated houses of the rich, the churches preparing their Christmas celebrations. In the house of Dostoyevsky's publisher Krayevsky, Mikhail's children were attending a Christmas party, their minds on presents and fun. Perhaps only Mikhail thought of his brother as the sledges passed by his house and then Krayevsky's, where the children played.

Fyodor wrote: 'We were taken past your flat and I saw Krayevsky's was all lit up. You had told me that they were having a Christmas party and that the children had gone there with Emilia Fedorovna and now by this house I felt cruelly despondent. I took my leave, as it were, of the children. I hated to leave them, and afterwards even years later, how often I thought of them, almost with tears in my eyes.'[4] The sledges pulled away from the city lights and took to the open road, heading towards the majestic Ural mountains, the great geographical barrier between European and Asian Russia. The hard journey had begun: nearly two thousand miles to cover in less than three weeks. It was bitterly cold, bleak and lonely — and it was Christmas Eve.

[1] Letter to Mikhail, December 1849, *Dostoevsky: A Self Portrait*, page 58.

[2] Reminiscences of A.P. Milyukov, 1848 to 1849, *The Letters of Fyodor Michailovitch Dostoyevsky to his Family and Friends*, page 280.

[3] Letter to Mikhail, February 1854, *Dostoevsky: A Self Portrait*, page 61.

[4] *Ibid*, page 62.

Chapter Seven
THE WIVES AT TOBOLSK

'It was a sad moment when we crossed the Urals. The horses and sledges had floundered into the drifts. A snow-storm was raging. We got out of the sledges — it was night — and stood waiting while they were dragged out of drifts. All around us was the snow and the storm; it was the frontier of Europe; ahead was Siberia and our unknown fate, while all the past lay behind us — it was so depressing that I was moved to tears.'[1]

The journey had been harsh and bitter. Dostoyevsky had had to sit in the freezing cold for ten hours at a time. Even though he had by this time been given a covered sledge, he was still frozen to the marrow. Even so, he had been luckier than many: prisoners often were forced to walk at least part of the way and, as a result, some died en route.

It was with mixed emotions that Dostoyevsky approached the great divide between Europe and Asia: relief because the journey was half over, apprehension at the unknown future, grief over what he had left behind. He was an urban European, a city-dweller, about to enter a great expanse of wild and underpopulated country. Gone were the stone buildings, the comforting log fires, the horses and carriages, the familiar faces of St Petersburg. Far away were his well-decorated, well-insulated rooms. Ahead lay the eastern steppes with their nomadic tribesmen, hunters and trappers, unfamiliar languages, hostile climate, a different dominant religion.

Most European Russians did not cross over to the Asian side unless they were exiled, punished, seeking adventure or sent there by the military or civil service. Imperial Russia was thus divided into two separate entities. In the fourteenth century Asian Russia had been dominant. Mongol armies had penetrated as far as the borders of Moscow and from their capital at Sarai their 'khan' had ruled the empire. But by the fifteenth century their empire had weakened; they were driven back to Asian Russia by the combined, although not allied, forces of Orthodox Muscovite Russia and the Turks, who conquered in the name of militant Islam. Consequently much of what was later to become Asian Russia was Turkish ruled and Muslim. Half the population of Semipalatinsk, the town where Dostoyevsky was to do his military service, was Muslim, as were several of his fellow convicts.

When Dostoyevsky was released from prison and allowed to write to his brother, among the many books he requested was the Koran. Four years in Eastern Russia had introduced him to the Islamic way and, while he never expressed any interest in following it, he was always interested in exploring other faiths.

In Asian Russia the Petrashevsky prisoners would encounter not only a different dominant religion but different races of people. Moving there as free men would have been challenging enough, but to go as middle-class prisoners, unused to physical hardship or discomfort, was daunting indeed. They were to exchange well-insulated well-decorated rooms for thin prison walls affording little protection from ferocious winter cold and sizzling summer heat.

The horrors of the life awaiting them seemed too great a misery for the younger of the two other prisoners who travelled with Dostoyevsky to Siberia. Jastrzenbski, sentenced to six years' hard labour and destined for a different prison from Durov and Dostoyevsky, was in despair. One night he announced that he had decided to kill himself. His life was in ruins — better to end it, he said.

His two companions went into action to cheer him up. Durov negotiated with the guards for some tea and Dostoyevsky produced some cigars he had hidden and saved. The three men talked long into the night. The atmosphere was congenial and their conversation did not dwell on the miseries they were to face. They merely enjoyed one another's companionship and conversation, aspects of life that could not be spoiled by imprisonment or the prospect of a dismal future. Their companionship blocked out the sights they had already seen, of prisoners chained to a wall unable to move, thus punished because of their dangerous temperaments. It blotted out too the sound of howls and drunken behaviour coming from the neighbouring cells of the prison in which they were temporarily housed. The three men who smoked and drank tea must have felt a little as though they were to be flung into the lions' den. They were not from the same class as most of the other prisoners, nor did they have the same physical strength. They could hope for little camaraderie with the peasants and common criminals and certainly could expect no welcome from anyone. However, as the night deepened and they grew warm with the tea and cigars, Jastrzenbski changed his mind. He still had no illusions about what was to come but he felt able to face it. Dostoyevsky's calm acceptance of his own fate soothed the younger man, and he parted with his friends in a much better humour. Jastrzenbski went on to serve and survive his sentence and lived to tell the story of that night.

Now that Dostoyevsky and Durov had arrived at Tobolsk they were to make their last contact for four years with others from European Russia who valued freedom of thought and justice. Dostoyevsky wrote to his brother Mikhail: 'I wish I could tell you in detail of our six days in Tobolsk and the impressions they left on me, but this isn't the right place. I will only say that the sympathy and lively concern we met with blessed us with almost complete happiness. The exiles of the old days (that is, not they themselves but their wives) looked after us as though we were their own flesh and blood. What wonderful people, tried by twenty-five years of sorrow and self-sacrifice! We had only a glimpse of them, for we were strictly confined. But they sent us food and clothing, they consoled us and gave us courage.'[2]

These 'exiles of the old days' were the Decembrists who had challenged Nicholas I when he first came to the throne. Dostoyevsky knew of their rebellion and fate, and in some ways the aims of the Petrashevsky and Durov circles were not dissimilar. They were in a way taking up the anthem. The Decembrists themselves had been officers of the army who had tried to educate the whole army, unsuccessfully, and persuade them to rise against Tsarism. The death of Alexander I caught them by surprise: an empty throne and a hesitating Grand Duke was too good an opportunity to miss. However they were able to gather only three thousand men in the Senate Square and when the Tsar had tried to disperse the uprising without bloodshed they shot his negotiator dead. The Tsar was forced to fire on the protesters and they fled to carry on a sporadic but doomed revolution.

The Decembrists are considered by many historians to be the first precursors of organized revolution in Russia. This was not the first time the government in Russia had been challenged by its own people. Russian history was scattered with uprisings and mutinies, and the Decembrists may have been just another such mutiny. But the Decembrist uprising was the first to possess a manifesto. Their rebellion was not motivated by dissatisfaction with a senior officer or by lousy pay. They had thought through a political agenda that would serve the people and make Russia a better place. Their demands were not for themselves but for the people. Despite their noble ideals, however, they had no popular support.

After the uprising was crushed the sentences given out were execution for five men, exile for life for some, and hard labour or lesser periods in Siberia.

When the survivors were sent to Siberia their wives followed. It was some of these women who now, at Tobolsk, Dostoyevsky's last major stop before prison, persuaded the authorities to let them meet with the prisoners and cook them some hot food. Among them was Natalya Fonvizina, an educated woman with a great love of literature. Dostoyevsky struck up a friendship with her that he was to maintain through correspondence in future years.

Besides food the women gave each prisoner a copy of the New Testament, the only book they were allowed to possess in prison and one that Dostoyevsky was to treasure for the rest of his life. During the four years in prison it was virtually his only reading matter, and when he died, thirty-one years later, it was clasped in his hands. When he left prison he wrote to Natalya Fonvizina describing to her something of the faith that he had rediscovered, perhaps partly through his many readings of that New Testament.

The Decembrists' wives' ministrations were not only of the spiritual kind. Inside each book jacket they slipped a ten rouble note to give the prisoners some bargaining power when they arrived. They also provided information about the prison to which Dostoyevsky and Durov were going. The governor, they said, was a reasonable man, but they must watch out for Major Krivtsov. He was a drunkard and a thug, given to punishing and beating prisoners at whim. Dostoyevsky did indeed, come across this man and some have suggested that a punishment by the Major caused Dostoyevsky's first major epileptic fit, although the story of the punishment itself is more likely to be rumour than fact, as Dostoyevsky himself does not refer to it directly.

The wives also arranged that the prisoners should be carried by coach to their gaol and not risk death by walking in the bitter Siberian cold. They promised too that they would write a letter to the governor of the prison requesting that these prisoners be given the courtesy due to their station. Unfortunately their letter arrived at the same time as one from the Tsar's office stating that under no circumstances were these prisoners to be given any special treatment. The governor had little choice in the matter.

The meeting with the Decembrists' wives was over all too soon and Dostoyevsky and Durov were taken through the driving snow to Omsk and their prison. As they left the town, Natalya Fonvizina and a companion made their way to the road where they had arranged with the sleigh driver to let them meet once more. The two men said one last farewell before ascending their sleigh again and, watched by the two figures wrapped tightly against the subzero cold, they disappeared into the white of the steppe.

[1] Letter to Mikhail, February 1854, *Dostoevsky: A Self Portrait*, pages 62 and 63.

[2] *Ibid*, page 63.

Chapter Eight
THE 'UNFORTUNATES'

Dostoyevsky's prison term was a turning-point in his life. Such was the change in his circumstances — from minor noble and famous author to commoner stripped of all privileges, including liberty — that a change in his outlook was almost inevitable. In later years he was to trace many of his views about the Russian people and their faith to what he learned in prison. In Siberia he was compelled to live in close proximity with people he would never normally have met. This forced an unexpected comradeship on him and effected a profound change in his attitudes, not only in his philosophical thought but also in his faith.

Nevertheless, the change may have been more of a re-evaluation than reversal. It is easy to interpret such sudden and dramatic events in his life as a landmark as important to Dostoyevsky as his conversion on the road to Damascus was to St Paul. However, although Dostoyevsky would now reassess what he believed, much of what he came to espouse in later years had its foundations in his life before prison. According to his doctor friend, Stepan Yanovsky, he had continued to practise his religion throughout the time that the Petrashevsky circle led him into a revolutionary conspiracy.

Dostoyevsky arrived at Omsk gaol with a mixture of beliefs. Rather than provoking a conversion, Siberia perhaps acted as a catalyst on his thought processes. When he left prison, his letters and early works still sound like someone searching for a creed, rather than someone who believes he has found the answer. However, his immediate task was to survive his new status as prisoner and peasant, not to plan for the future. He could do no more than hope that his old privileges and life would one day be restored and that then he would have the opportunity to assess and absorb what he was learning.

The circumstances of Dostoyevsky's confinement were so dramatic that the urge to use them as material for a book was irresistible. In many of his novels he portrayed parts of his own life's story and even parodied his friends and colleagues. Nowhere is this autobiographical detail more apparent than in the short novel many consider his first masterpiece, *The House of the Dead*, an account of his time in prison. Censorship rules prohibited his simply writing and publishing a straightforward account of what had happened to him in prison, but he wanted to use what he had seen and suffered, to give readers a chance to experience the reality of being an 'unfortunate', as the prisoners were called by the local residents. By writing a novel rather than a journalistic account, he was able to get his book published without offending the censors and thereby jeopardizing his chances of publishing again.

The House of the Dead was published in 1860, over a decade after Dostoyevsky was first put in chains. The book deals clearly with the subject of his prison years, without breaking the censorship laws. It uses a simple fictional device. The narrator discovers in the belongings of a recently dead convict a manuscript describing that convict's time in gaol. The convict, Alexander Petrovitch, had been convicted of murdering his wife and sentenced to ten years in prison in Siberia. The crime is different, the sentence is longer; but, once the narrative begins, the experiences described are those of Fyodor Dostoyevsky.

'Fearfully I raise my head and in the fitful candlelight gaze at my slumbering companions. I watch their unhappy countenances, their miserable beds. I view their nakedness, their wretchedness, and then convince myself that it is no nightmare but simple reality. Yes, it is reality. I hear a groan. Someone has moved his arm and caused his chains to rattle. Another is troubled in his dreams and speaks aloud, while the old grandfather prays for the "Orthodox Christians". I listen to his prayer, uttered regularly in soft, rather drawling tones: "Lord Jesus Christ, have mercy on us."'[1]

The book did not break the censorship laws, but its readers understood that the story was based on Dostoyevsky's own.

In fact, as Dostoyevsky commented years later, some people still believed that he himself had been exiled for murdering his wife.

There were fifteen hundred posts in the prison fence at Omsk, and the prisoners used them to count off the days of their confinement. When a prisoner had counted them all, there was cause for great celebration. Prison conditions were hardly bearable. Thirty men were locked up in one long barrack room for the duration of the hours of darkness. Their beds were boards and they had little protection from the heat or severe cold. For the winter they were issued sheepskin coats which they wore during the day and slept under at night. The room was full of smoke and dirt, and it stank. The cold in winter was so severe that the one stove they had in the barracks could not thaw the ice on the windows which was always three inches thick. Looking back on it, Dostoyevsky was surprised that he ever got used to these conditions.

The food, he remarked in *The House of the Dead*, was not so bad and the hard labour was not cruelly inflicted. He endured no individual torture, either physical or mental, and it is unlikely that he suffered any extra punishment. Other Petrashevskyites were treated as political prisoners, but in Omsk gaol Dostoyevsky was a common criminal. His prison was not like the labour camps more recently portrayed in the novels of Alexander Solzhenitsyn, nor did he suffer either the brutality meted out in the 1970s and 80s to Anatoly (now Nathan) Sheransky or the indignity of a psychiatric ward.

Nevertheless, to suffer the deprivation of liberty, in a place where the temperature can reach forty degrees below freezing, to be deprived of the opportunity to write and, most important for Dostoyevsky, never, never to be left alone — this was harsh punishment indeed for the crime of reading out a letter and planning to buy a printing press.

Perhaps the hardest part of prison life for Dostoyevsky was the constant companionship of other prisoners. Thus, for example: 'could I ever have imagined the poignant and terrible suffering of never being alone even for one minute during ten years? Working under escort in the barracks together with two hundred "companions": never alone, never!'[2] So said Alexander Petrovitch in *The*

House of the Dead. For Dostoyevsky himself it was of course four years.

Occasionally the guards took the prisoners for a steam bath. The prisoners sat or stood tightly packed in a steaming room. Dostoyevsky was found a seat, which he had to pay for, next to a fellow prisoner. This is what he saw: 'The common people do not care to wash with soap and water; they prefer the horrible method of stewing and then douching themselves with cold water. Below I could see fifty bundles of twigs rising and falling; the holders were whipping themselves into a state akin to intoxication. The steam became thicker and thicker every minute, so that what one now felt was not a warm but a burning sensation, as from boiling pitch. The convicts shouted and howled to the accompaniment of the hundred chains shaking on the floor . . . It seemed to me that if ever we met in hell we should be reminded of this place.'[3]

Dostoyevsky was one of only a few noblemen in the prison. Until he arrived there he had no idea how hostile the peasant classes and serfs were towards noblemen, however humble: 'Their hatred for the nobility is boundless; they regard all of us who belong to it with hostility and enmity. They would have devoured us if only they could.'[4] The peasants did not ask why such men were in prison; they saw all noblemen as oppressors and held them each personally responsible for the exploitation of the peasants.

One of the other noblemen was a prince, accused of having brutally murdered his father. The evidence against him was overwhelming; all of his local community was convinced that he did it and he was serving a long sentence for the crime. To Dostoyevsky, however, he seemed incapable of committing such a crime, and the prince himself claimed that he was innocent. Years later, after a copy of *The House of the Dead* had reached someone who knew of the case, Dostoyevsky learned that the prince had finally been vindicated. Another man confessed to the crime and the prince was released, but the best years of his life were gone. In Dostoyevsky's last novel, *The Brothers Karamazov*, one brother suffers such a fate. The evidence that he murdered his father is overwhelming and all those around him believe he committed the crime. Dmitry Karamazov is punished for what he did not do.

Apart from the prince and a few others Dostoyevsky had little noble company, and his relationships with the other men were always precarious. Work assignments, especially at the beginning of his sentence, were where the difficulties were most apparent. The convicts, though they did as little work as they could get away with, did not welcome help from a nobleman. Instead they behaved like a gang of school children who have decided to ostracize one of their number. Early in his sentence, Dostoyevsky was sent with a party of convicts to dismantle a barge. This task was performed slowly until the convicts were told they could go back to the barracks as soon as it was done. Then, said Dostoyevsky, the convicts became suddenly 'intelligent' and got on with their work efficiently and quickly. As for him, however, 'I seemed all the time to be in somebody's way . . . ' A barrage of unhelpful and mocking remarks was flung at him. He was told to 'clear off' or 'get out of the light', sworn at and informed that he was not wanted. In the end he gave up and sat down. It was no comfort that he had had a restful day, for prison was going to be bearable only if he could make friends with the men, or at least be tolerated by them. Dostoyevsky kept no company with his fellow Petrashevskyite, Durov, either, and fellow prisoners assumed that the two hated each other.

Those who remembered serving time with Dostoyevsky had contradictory memories of him. Some remembered him as a withdrawn grumpy man who kept to himself. One described him as a 'wolf in a trap':[5] others recalled him as a popular soul and the producer of the prison play. Probably both descriptions are accurate: Dostoyevsky found the fact he was never alone very trying and withdrew into himself, but he also produced the play, which turned out to be a great success; some of the prisoners' performances, Dostoyevsky claimed, were the best he had ever seen.

He made a few individual friends in prison, although not always on the terms he would have liked. One man adopted him as his master and took pains to serve him tea and generally look after his needs — while robbing him incessantly. This erratic behaviour and other similar examples of capriciousness no doubt contributed to a change in Dostoyevsky's philosophy of humankind: he came to prison a martyr for a socialist cause, convinced that people are fundamentally good, made evil by their environment. A man who was beaten, starved, unjustly treated and denied access to a better life could not be held responsible for his character. Given better circumstances, he would be a better man; if food, good treatment, education and justice were made equally available to all, then strife and warfare would disappear.

When Dostoyevsky left prison, he was no longer a socialist. Having observed the behaviour of disadvantaged men at close quarters he concluded that evil came from the inner man, not his environment: 'During many years I never remarked the least sign of repentance nor even the slightest uneasiness in a man with regard to his crime, and that most of the convicts considered neither honour nor conscience, holding that they had a right to act as they thought fit. Certainly vanity, bad example, deceitfulness, and false shame were responsible for much. On the other hand, who can claim to have sounded the depths of those hearts given over to perdition, and to have found them closed to all light? It would seem indeed that during all those years I should have been able to detect some indication, however fugitive, of some regret, of some moral suffering. I positively saw nothing of the kind.'[6]

This is not to say that Dostoyevsky lost his faith in justice or his desire to fight for fair treatment for all human beings, but the philosophy that had been at the centre of his socialist thinking collapsed. No longer could he believe in the man who would willingly be unenvious, loving and content in one of Fourier's phalansteries. Dostoyevsky had come to believe in a fallen race.

His prison experience also made him more critical of the penal system. Prison, he said, was not an effective means of rehabilitation: a prison term does more to reassure society than to benefit the prisoner. Hard labour only reinforces feelings of hatred, pride and anger. The only 'rehabilitation' that the inmates themselves wanted was to find ways to make money, most of which they spent on drink. 'The convict is greedy for money, to the point of madness, and if he throws it away he does so in order to procure what he values far above money — liberty or at least some semblance of liberty.'[7] Convicts thought up all sorts of ways to make it. Even the prison dogs were not safe: one very endearing animal friend of Dostoyevsky finished up as the lining in a pair of boots that were sold to the wife of a local official.

Dostoyevsky, then, gave up the idea of man as a 'noble savage', but he did not give up on the human race. Now, even though he believed that humanity is naturally sinful, he also came to love and respect the common people much more than he had before. Even though he withdrew from many of those around him because he deplored their behaviour, he saw in them a simple unquestioning faith that he came to believe was the essence of salvation.

Very little was sacred among the prisoners, but Dostoyevsky noticed that they respected each other's religions. When they took part in church rituals they did so with respect and dignity in contrast to their often petty and drunken behaviour. In *The House of the Dead* Dostoyevsky recalls the way the prisoners prostrated themselves with fervour at Lenten services.[8] They placed particular faith in the fact that Jesus had saved the thief on the cross. Dostoyevsky watched them as each went forward with his farthing to give for the collection or for a candle. Through their actions and their piety they seemed to say, 'I too am a man.' He speculated that as they said their prayers, not only before God but before the noblemen and the free men of the town, they may have said, 'Before God we are all equal.'

Of the services themselves he wrote, 'The Lenten services, familiar to me from early childhood in my father's house — the solemn prayers, the protestations — all stirred in me the memory of things long, long past, and awoke my earliest impressions to fresh life.'[9]

In prison, nevertheless, holy days and feast days were not happily anticipated. The men drank, gambled and brawled their way through their time off, and the guards kept clear of them as they grew steadily drunker and more argumentative. Dostoyevsky wrote of one holiday: 'I could never understand how it was that within five minutes of the governor's departure the room was full of drunken men, all of whom had appeared stone-cold sober as long as he remained.'[10] Drunkenness often turned to violence. After one particularly brutal Easter-day brawl, he records in his *Diary of a Writer*, he went back to his barrack room and lay down on his bunk feigning sleep to avoid being bothered by fellow prisoners. As he lay there he remembered that summer's day in Darovoye when he ran for comfort to the peasant for fear of the wolf. Marey's kindness to him that long-ago day showed him that, while a pleasant environment might not make a person righteous, a harsh environment did not necessarily make him evil. This realization left him with a basic tension in his view of human nature: people could do evil without provocation, but they could also do good in the face of provocation. His later portrayals of men such as Raskolnikov in *Crime and Punishment* illustrate this dilemma: in one man both tremendous evil and tremendous love can be expressed: in one world both destruction and salvation are at work.

He was not necessarily conscious of these changes in his world-view while he was still in prison. It was with hindsight that Dostoyevsky came to terms with much of what he had learned in prison and organized it into a coherent creed.

[1] *The House of the Dead*, page 164.

[2] *Ibid*, page 9.

[3] *Ibid*, pages 121–22.

[4] Letter to Mikhail, 22 February 1854, *The Letters of Fyodor Michailovitch Dostoyevsky to his Family and Friends*, page 59.

[5] From the Memoranda of P.K. Martyanov, *The Letters of Fyodor Michailovitch Dostoyevsky to his Family and Friends*, page 285.

[6] *The House of the Dead*, page 14.

[7] *Ibid*, page 80.

[8] *Ibid*, page 228.

[9] *Ibid*, page 227.

[10] *Ibid*, page 136.

Chapter Nine
FREEDOM IN EXILE

'One afternoon, when the drum beat for work, they took the eagle, tied his beak (for he assumed a desperate attitude), and took him out on to the ramparts. The twelve convicts forming the gang were extremely anxious to know where he would go. It was a strange thing; they all seemed as happy as though they had themselves obtained their freedom.'[1]

Dostoyevsky received a form of freedom in February 1854 but, although his prison sentence was completed, his punishment was not. In March of that year he was given the rank of private and was sent to join the Seventh Siberian Regiment in Semipalatinsk, an outpost town close to the Russo-Chinese border.

Semipalatinsk had a population of about six thousand, approximately half of whom were Muslim. Outside the town the Kirghizes, nomads of the steppe, camped, coming in to more permanent homes only during the winter months. There were seven mosques in the town, but only one church. As in most frontier towns, the people were hardened by their harsh living conditions, and money and self-interest dominated their lives. The Orthodox church seemed to have little relevance to their daily struggle to scratch a living out of the tundra.

In this difficult town, nicknamed 'The Devil's Sandbox', Dostoyevsky resumed his career in the army. His length of service had been set at four years but the confiscation of his civil rights was indefinite. Dostoyevsky had a long way to go before he could call himself a free man.

His first act on leaving prison was to write to his brother Mikhail in St Petersburg. In this letter he first of all reproached his brother for not having answered his letters to him, not knowing whether to blame Mikhail for not replying, or to blame the authorities for intercepting or failing to deliver the letters.

He then told his brother all he could about the past four years, describing prison conditions and some of the difficulties he had suffered. Despite it all, he reassured Mikhail, he was still reasonably healthy and looking forward to his new start. Finally, and inevitably, he asked his brother to send him some books, including the Koran and Kant's *Critique of Reason*.

Dostoyevsky had been without books for almost four years, his only respite being the time spent in hospital. Sometimes he was genuinely sick but sometimes he got a little extra time in bed and a few books, courtesy of a sympathetic doctor. His enthusiasm to read overcame his repulsion at having to endure hospital routine and, most particularly, hospital garments: 'It (his dressing gown) exhaled a most offensive odour which contact with my body helped to bring out. It smelt of plasters and medicaments of all kinds, and seemed as though it had been worn by patients from time immemorial; the lining had, perhaps, been washed once, but I would not swear to it. Certainly at the time I put it on it was saturated with lotions and stained by contact with poultices and plasters of every imaginable kind.'[2]

Dostoyevsky devoured his reading matter secretly. Among other works, he read the novels of Charles Dickens, whom he greatly admired and with whom he is often compared. The two writers' descriptions of the living conditions of the urban poor had a similar impact on readers: for the first time the more affluent gained some insight into what it was like to be poor in Dostoyevsky's Russia or Dickens' London.

Dostoyevsky sent his first letter to Mikhail through unofficial channels because its contents gave away too much about prison conditions and it would have been intercepted and censored by the authorities if it had been posted in the ordinary way. (All Dostoyevsky's post was to be monitored for many years to come.) However, he asked Mikhail to reply through the normal post, probably in the hope that such a reply would take less time to arrive.

In Semipalatinsk Dostoyevsky was a prisoner on the outside.

He still wore the red cap showing he was a convict soldier. He still could not publish and he definitely could not leave Asian Russia. At first he lived in barracks with the other soldiers of the regiment, who were mostly peasants, exiles or convict soldiers like himself. There was little difference between these conditions and his environment in prison. However, very soon he got permission to live outside the barracks. He rented a small room in a house occupied by the landlady and her two daughters, who were most impressed that he had once been a nobleman, however minor. His room was a typical peasant dwelling with mud walls lined with benches, and faded calico curtains dividing the living area from the sleeping area. At the window, where dismal dark red curtains hung, some straggly geraniums grew. The room was lit by candles, which he had to use almost all the time because the small window let in little light, and it was infested with fleas. Despite all these drawbacks the accommodation had one major advantage over barracks: he could be alone there.

Dostoyevsky was not unsuited to the military life. His time at the Academy of Engineers had prepared him for parade drill, military discipline, nights on watch and exercises. Moreover, he was fitter now than he had ever been. Hard labour and rationed food had made him strong. Although he had suffered the stomach problems of almost every convict, his health had not broken. He was more fortunate than the others: Durov had suffered badly both physically and mentally and had hardly been able to walk when he left prison. Petrashevsky himself, Dostoyevsky wrote to his brother, was not in his right mind. Dostoyevsky, by contrast, was ready to start again and he faced the uncertainty of an indefinite period in Siberia with equanimity, even optimism.

He had left prison with many of his previous ideas about human nature, the role of socialism and the Christian faith broken down but he had not, as yet, begun to build any coherent belief system of his own. The society of Semipalatinsk did not urge him to intellectual activity. As an ex-convict Dostoyevsky was on a par with the commonest peasant, and few educated people were willing to give him the time of day during those first few months. To continue his education Dostoyevsky depended on the parcels and letters he received from home. He also took the opportunity to write to Natalya Fonvizina to thank her for the New Testament that she had given him at Tobolsk and which he still treasured. She was a religious woman and well educated, and he felt that he could tell her about his emerging faith. In his letter, he started to come to terms with and analyze the changes in his ideas and faith.

His time in prison with the New Testament as virtually his only reading matter had given him a chance to reassess the character and claims of Jesus Christ. 'I believe that there is nothing lovelier, deeper, more sympathetic, more rational, more manly and more perfect than the Saviour', he wrote. 'I say to myself with jealous love that there is no one else like Him, but that there could be none. I would even say more: If anyone could prove to me that Christ is outside the truth and if the truth really did exclude Christ, I should prefer to stay with Christ and not with the truth.'[3]

Even so, this comment in his letter to Natalya Fonvizina is hard to fathom and is, in some ways, controversial. It is probable that he was searching for a new creed. He had found socialist and utopian theories inadequate in the face of human evil. He had also come to believe that claims to possess 'absolute truth' were dangerous because a definition of absolute morality somehow bound Christ and God to obey it.

In Dostoyevsky's view, most religious creeds or 'absolute truths' were flawed. In Christ, by contrast, Dostoyevsky saw a perfect man who had given the world a great philosophy. In his life and teaching Christ combined all the justice, love and strength that was required of humankind. Christ's teaching seemed to work in the real world and, where a set creed might fail, Christ's character was still credible. It seemed more important to come to know and love the Saviour than to adhere to a creed purporting to be the truth.

Much of Dostoyevsky's later work was to deal with this very conflict between absolute morality and the unfathomable character of God. In one potent scene in *The Brothers Karamazov*, for example, Alyosha and Ivan discuss the morality of God. Alyosha asks Ivan if he could build the most beautiful building in the world, if he knew beforehand that it would entail the death of a child. The brothers both decide that they could not do so and yet this is what they charge God with doing: he, with full foreknowledge, has created a world in which many children die. Absolute morality would suggest that such a venture was not worth the suffering it caused, but loyalty to God might require accepting that suffering.

In 1854, though, Dostoyevsky was not so preoccupied by philosophy: he had become enamoured with Christ, but he was still living through the suffering that was to make his later novels deal so candidly with eternal questions. Whether or not he did as yet believe Christ to be divine or accept him as his own Saviour, in the personal, evangelical sense, is unclear. However, the effect his years in prison may have had on his philosophy of life and personal psychology is important.

It is a well-known technique in mind-bending that if a person is subject to a complete change in his personal circumstances, if everything that was once secure and familiar is taken away, if everything that once appeared normal becomes abnormal, the subject becomes more vulnerable to suggestion. Psychological torturers know that if all the conditioning and norms by which people live their lives are taken away, careful suggestion can replace the old ideas with new ones and so, literally, change the subject's mind. Whether this change of mind is permanent is debatable. However it does seem that 'conversion' can occur when the subject loses all familiar points of reference (home, family, job, country . . .), as Dostoyevsky did, and has to build a new life using new points of reference.

It is not surprising then that some changes in his psychology may have taken place and that he enthusiastically embraced the teaching of Christ when he got out of prison. This can be used to explain Dostoyevsky's commitment to Christ — for some, especially readers and writers in Communist Russia, an inconvenient blot on an otherwise pure revolutionary career. Others, however, feel that only a major conversion can adequately account for his change in beliefs. For many, the reasons — psychological or divine — are irrelevant. His change of heart is seen as the gradual change and development in ideas of a brilliant man subjected to tragedy and cruelty. Whatever the explanation, only time would tell whether his change of mind was also a change of heart.

Not long after his release into the army, his loneliness was alleviated. A companion from the familiar world of European Russia arrived. Baron Alexander Wrangel was a person with whom Dostoyevsky could speak on level terms and with whom he could develop a friendship. In December 1849 this young man, then seventeen years old, had stood in Semyonovsky Square and watched the mock execution. He had read Dostoyevsky's work and felt deeply for the writer as he witnessed the trick perpetrated on the conspirators. While Dostoyevsky served his sentence Baron Wrangel embarked on his career as a public prosecutor. Like many young men he wanted to travel and he applied for a transfer to Semipalatinsk. That way he could combine his quest for adventure with an opportunity to meet the writer he admired.

He went first to Mikhail to pick up books, letters and gossip, and as soon as he arrived in Semipalatinsk he sent for Dostoyevsky. He describes their first meeting: 'At first he did not know who I was and why I had asked him to come; so he was in the beginning very reticent. He wore a grey military cloak with a high red collar and red epaulettes; his pale, freckled face had a morose expression. His fair hair was closely shorn. He scrutinized me keenly with his intelligent blue-grey eyes, as if seeking to divine what sort of person I was.'[4]

Both men recalled the meeting vividly. Dostoyevsky, nervous at being called to the district attorney's office, thought he might be in some sort of trouble. Wrangel, on the other hand, was deeply apprehensive at the thought of meeting this great but tragic figure and could only hope that they might like each other. Wrangel offered him the letters he had brought from home and Dostoyevsky sat down and read them. The atmosphere was now more relaxed since Wrangel had explained himself, but as Dostoyevsky read the letters he began to cry. It was perhaps not only the letters but the fact that, for the first time in four years, he had been treated with respect. His tears moved his young admirer who also had some letters from home which he began to read. In a moment they were both crying: the young man far from home and facing a new independent life, and the older man not knowing whether he would ever see his family again. From that day on the two men were firm friends.

Baron Wrangel's arrival changed Dostoyevsky's life in the small frontier town. Suddenly he was no longer *persona non grata*. Under the young baron's guidance and through his introductions he was accepted into the higher society of Semipalatinsk, such as it was. The friendship of the two men did not go unnoticed by the authorities but, despite initial suspicion, they interfered little. 'I grew fonder and fonder of Dostoyevsky', wrote the baron; 'my house was open to him day and night. When I returned from duty, I often found him there already having come to me from the drill-ground or the regimental office.'[5]

Baron Wrangel was a man of traditional Christian faith. At that time, Dostoyevsky was not a great church-goer. He had no respect for the Siberian priests and not much more respect for the priests of European Russia. Neither did he and the baron speak much about it: 'He seldom spoke of religion. He was at heart religious, though he rarely entered a church; the popes, and especially the Siberian ones, he could not stand at all. Of Christ he would speak with moving rapture.'[6]

Again it was Christ rather than easily flawed man-made institutions that attracted him. Having assented once to a philosophy with too much haste, Dostoyevsky was cautious now that he was rebuilding his life and beliefs.

Baron Wrangel rented a small cottage outside the town for the summer. As often as he could get away the two men retreated to the cottage, where Dostoyevsky gardened assiduously. He managed to grow dahlias and carnations, difficult to do on the tundra. 'I can see Dostoyevsky now, watering the young plants', wrote the baron; 'he would take off his regimental cloak, and stand among the flower-beds in a pink cotton shirt . . . He was quite fascinated with gardening and took great delight in it.'[7]

Baron Wrangel loved riding and after much persuasion managed to convince Dostoyevsky to learn. He was a bit awkward on horseback at first but once he got used to it he enjoyed their rides on the steppe. Riding gave him a feeling of freedom.

The gentlemen at the house even received the occasional lady visitor. They also encouraged two snakes to come by putting out milk for them, although the snakes did not mix well with the ladies. Friendship, a hot summer, some chances to read, write and discuss life — these went a long way towards improving Dostoyevsky's state of mind. By now he was thirty-three and had been a long time out of the regular company of women.

His rehabilitation may have been going smoothly but he would soon run into trouble again, this time of the emotional kind. Dostoyevsky fell in love.

[1] *The House of the Dead*, page 252.

[2] *Ibid*, page 171.

[3] Letter to Natalya Fonvizina, March 1854, *The Letters of Fyodor Michailovitch Dostoyevsky to his Family and Friends*, page 71.

[4] Reminiscences of Baron Alexander Wrangel, *The Letters of Fyodor Michailovitch Dostoyevsky to his Family and Friends*, page 291.

[5] *Ibid*, pages 296–97.

[6] *Ibid*, page 304.

[7] *Ibid*, page 301.

Chapter Ten
LOVE AND MARRIAGE

Maria Isayeva was twenty-eight when Dostoyevsky first met her. She was married to a drunk, Alexander Isayev, who was attempting to hold down a job as a customs official in the Russian civil service. Although Alexander Isayev was not actually cruel to his wife, his heavy drinking reduced the couple to near poverty. The couple's son, Pasha, was seven years old.

Dostoyevsky later portrayed Alexander Isayev in *Crime and Punishment* through the comical if tragic figure of Marmeladov: 'He was a man over fifty, bald and grizzled, of medium height, and stoutly built. His face, bloated from continual drinking, was of a yellow, even greenish, tinge, with swollen eyelids, out of which keen, reddish eyes gleamed like little chinks.'[1] Although Marmeladov may not be an exact copy of Isayev, his drunken behaviour led to the death of his wife, the consumptive Katerina Ivanova (believed to be a portrait of Maria) just as Alexander's brought down his wife, Maria, already showing signs of the tuberculosis that was to claim her.

Baron Wrangel, who watched the relationship between Dostoyevsky and Maria develop, had no great respect for Maria whom he regarded as capricious and jealous. Had he realized how seriously Dostoyevsky was in love with her he might have made more effort to help him avoid a mistake. Thinking this was only a casual flirtation, he was persuaded by Dostoyevsky to connive in the couple's meetings. More than once he got Isayev drunk to keep him out of their way.

Wrangel, however, saw immediately what turned out to be the fatal flaw in the relationship. What Dostoyevsky took for love was

Maria's pity for him as an ex-convict. Perhaps she also encouraged him because she needed affection, something of which she got little enough from Alexander Isayev. 'I do not think that she highly esteemed him,' Wrangel later wrote as he recalled the couple's initial meetings; 'it was more that she pitied him. Possibly she was attached to him also; but in love with him she most decidedly never was.'[2]

Wrangel reports that Maria said Dostoyevsky was a man with no future. She felt sorry for this writer who had once been famous, who was now reduced to living in little more than a hut in Siberia and who still faced at least a four-year stretch in the army and an indefinite period in Siberia. She underestimated Dostoyevsky's tenacity in regaining his civil rights, getting out of Siberia and winning her hand.

This was not the first time Dostoyevsky had been in love, nor was it the first time he had mistaken fondness and affection for something deeper. It was not even the first time he ignored the fact that the object of his affection was already married. Avdotya Panayeva, wife of Ivan Panayev, had been a society hostess in St Petersburg when Dostoyevsky was enjoying his fame after publishing *Poor Folk*. She was his ideal woman, both beautiful and clever, and it was well known that her marriage was a little lacking in lustre. Her husband's infidelity gave many men, including Dostoyevsky, the hope that she might look in their direction for comfort. She was kind to him and she probably liked him, but she was not in love with him.

Dostoyevsky's infatuation, on the other hand, was evident, and his inexperience and uncertainty led to bouts of over-confident arrogance combined with nervous confusion. His hopes were never fulfilled and soon after this first passion Dostoyevsky was to find himself in gaol, separated from regular female company for nearly five years. It is not surprising that upon his release Dostoyevsky was quick to fall in love and tempted to interpret any affection he got in return as a mutual passion, especially when Maria's loneliness and ill-treatment at the hands of her husband made her crave the affection Dostoyevsky offered.

At first the affair consisted only of visits to the Isayevs' dwelling, where intense fraternization took place. The desperation of their situation made Dostoyevsky love Maria more, and made her more grateful for his attention and generosity.

Then a great blow was inflicted on the relationship: the Isayevs moved from Semipalatinsk to Kuznetsk some four hundred miles away. Alexander Isayev had got a job as a caretaker of an inn, which promised a new start for the family. Dostoyevsky was devastated. The restriction laid on him by the army meant that he would not be free to visit very often, if ever. There was a heart-rending farewell at which Baron Wrangel got Isayev too drunk to notice the passionate parting that took place between his wife and Dostoyevsky.

Dostoyevsky, desperate that Maria had gone, gave up working on *The House of the Dead* and began to consult a fortune-teller. The idea of another dimension of spiritual beings fascinated him, and the thought that he might discover what the future held for him was very tempting. His life thus far had been an indiscriminate mixture of success and disaster; if he could learn what was to come perhaps he could better prepare for it. In later life he was unequivocally to renounce his interest in any kind of spiritualism or occult practices, but for the moment all he wanted to know was whether there was any future for him and Maria, and he did not care how he found out.

He felt he could not live without her and her letters to him did not help him to bear their separation. She described in detail her poverty, Isayev's drunkenness and the fact he was in increasingly bad health. Dostoyevsky sent Maria money and wrote soothing letters to her but this was not enough. Once again he involved Wrangel in deception so that he could see Maria. This time Wrangel told Dostoyevsky's army superiors that Dostoyevsky was ill, while Dostoyevsky travelled half-way to Kuznetsk where he had arranged to meet Maria. When he arrived, however, she was not there. She had sent a message to say that she was nursing her sick husband and could not come. In fact the combination of sickness, drunkenness and despair finally proved too much for Alexander Isayev, and not long after Dostoyevsky received a letter saying that he had died.

Now Dostoyevsky had new hope but no way of consolidating his advantage, for Maria was in Kuznetsk and he was in Semipalatinsk.

He feared that she would fall in love with someone else — as, of course, she did.

Dostoyevsky's first rival was a fictitious wealthy official, of whom Maria wrote to make him jealous. His second rival was no fiction but a schoolmaster, younger than both of them but with a regular salary. He did not drink and was probably more suited to the ailing, selfish Maria and her son than was Dostoyevsky. Letters to Dostoyevsky describing this man and her affection for him sent Dostoyevsky shooting out of Semipalatinsk to Kuznetsk on an illegal diversion from military business to dissuade her from marrying the schoolmaster.

In February 1855, while Dostoyevsky was preoccupied with his affairs of the heart, something significant happened that was to give him the opportunity he sought to restart his career: Tsar Nicholas I died. Though he died as the Crimean War was being lost and had resolved none of Russia's internal injustices, such as serfdom, his death was a glimmer of hope for Dostoyevsky. Perhaps now he could appeal to a more merciful Tsar who had no personal involvement in his case. Rumours spread that there might be an amnesty for political prisoners granted by the new Tsar Alexander II, who was reputed to be more liberal. As soon as they heard the news, in March, Dostoyevsky and Baron Wrangel attended a solemn mass for Nicholas.

Nicholas I's death prompted Dostoyevsky to send the first of many missives to those in authority in European Russia, pleading his case for the right to publish and to return to European Russia. First he sent a poem dedicated to Nicholas's wife, the Tsarina, and expounding the virtues of her late husband. Then he wrote a poem on the coronation of the new Tsar. Both poems were unashamedly flattering; both intended to prove that Dostoyevsky would now use his writing talent to the benefit and not the detriment of the Tsarist regime.

To General Eduard Totlebon, the engineer hero of the siege of Sevastopol, and brother of an old flatmate of Dostoyevsky, he wrote: 'I was guilty, and am very conscious of it. I was convicted of the intention (but only the intention) of acting against the Government. I was lawfully and quite justly condemned; the hard, painful experiences of the ensuing years have sobered me, and altered my views in many respects.'[3]

Soon after the Tsar's death, Baron Wrangel's term of duty as district attorney expired and he had to return to European Russia. This meant that Dostoyevsky had a friend and ally pleading his cause in St Petersburg but it also meant that he was, once again, alone in Siberia. 'Our parting grieved me bitterly,' wrote Wrangel. 'I was young, strong, and full of roseate hopes; while he — great, God-given writer — was losing his only friend, and had to stay behind as a common soldier, sick, forsaken, desolate — in Siberia.'[4]

The letter to Totlebon had an effect though, and in the autumn of 1856 Dostoyevsky was promoted to second lieutenant and given permission to commence writing with a view to publication, as long as what he wrote came within the law. This was good progress and gave the lie to Maria's perception of Dostoyevsky as a man without a future. In 1857 he published a short story written in the Peter and Paul Fortress some years before, and in 1859 two novels, *Uncle's Dream* and *The Village of Stepanchikovo*, were published. He had established that he could once again get into print.

Just as persistence earned him the right to publish, it also won him the hand of Maria Isayeva in marriage. The wedding took place on 6 February 1857 in Kuznetsk. By now, however, this was a hollow victory. Fyodor was worn out with the battle and Maria was ill. Within days Maria was witness to Dostoyevsky's most severe epileptic fit to date.

The history of Dostoyevsky's epilepsy is not entirely clear, and many writers have speculated about it: for instance, whether the epilepsy manifested itself in childhood, was brought on by some shock, was the result of a congenital fault, or was a combination of both. Freud believed that it was hysterical and nervous, but one of Dostoyevsky's sons died as a result of similar convulsions, which would indicate a physical and inherited disorder. There is little evidence for major episodes in Dostoyevsky's childhood and early youth, but his flatmate Dmitry Grigorovich's description of his convulsions indicates that the disease already existed early on in Dostoyevsky's youth.

'Sometimes he would even have a fit on one of our few walks together. Once we chanced to come on a funeral. Dostoevsky insisted on turning back at once; but he had scarcely gone a few steps when he had such a violent fit that I was obliged to carry him, with the help of some passers-by, into the nearest shop; it was with great difficulty that we restored him to consciousness.'[5] One story, probably apocryphal, said that Dostoyevsky had a fit as a result of a severe flogging in prison. Dostoyevsky, however, never referred to this, although on one occasion, possibly because of a convulsion, he had to be confined to bed. This angered the notorious Major Krivtsov and Dostoyevsky was only just rescued from a flogging by a more conscientious officer. This story could be the source of the rumour that Dostoyevsky's epilepsy began in prison as a result of cruelty.

Whatever the origin of his convulsions, there is no doubt that later in life Dostoyevsky was plagued by them. He endowed many of his characters with epilepsy, including Prince Myshkin, hero of *The Idiot*, whose life is saved from a murderous attack by a conveniently timed epileptic fit. Dostoyevsky's descriptions of Myshkin's epilepsy give insight into how he viewed his affliction; Anna, his second wife, describes vividly how it appeared to others. This is how one seizure began: 'Suddenly he broke off in mid-syllable, turned white, started to get up from the couch and began leaning over toward me. I looked in amazement at his changed face. And suddenly there was a horrible, inhuman scream, or more precisely, a howl — and he began to topple forward.'[6]

The practical effects of his epilepsy, apart from the ever-present fear of having a seizure in the street or injuring himself severely during a fit, were the depression, confusion and loss of memory that followed. He lost more than one friend because he failed to recognize them after a fit. He wrote copious notes on the characterizations and plots of his novels so that he could remind himself of what he was working on if a seizure interrupted the flow.

Convulsions seemed to come haphazardly, although alcohol could provoke a fit and he thought certain types of weather also had an effect. Moreover he often knew when a fit was coming on, although he was helpless against it. One significant feature of his epilepsy was the feeling of ecstasy that immediately preceded a seizure: 'Then suddenly some gulf seemed to open up before him: a blinding *inner* light flooded his soul. The moment lasted perhaps half a second, yet he clearly and consciously remembered the beginning, the first sound of the dreadful scream, which burst from his chest of its own accord and which he could have done nothing to suppress. Then his consciousness was instantly extinguished and complete darkness set in.'[7]

His ill-health may have added some mysticism to Dostoyevsky's religious thought. Some Victorian artists (Coleridge was one) sought religious experiences through the use of drugs because they believed that drugs could break down the inhibitions of the rational mind and bring one closer to God; Dostoyevsky wondered whether his epilepsy could have the same effect. It no doubt coloured his vision of heaven but it did not cure him of the fear of death. All his life he feared sudden death brought on by a convulsion.

To his new wife, Maria, his epileptic seizure was terrifying. Not only had she married an ex-convict, she had married one with a severe brain disease. She had never seen anything like his fit before and she contacted doctors immediately, thus alerting the authorities to his medical condition. Epilepsy was officially diagnosed and Dostoyevsky was released from the army on grounds of ill-health.

Two years after his marriage, in 1857, after further appeals Dostoyevsky's noble title was restored to him. By July 1859 he was given permission to leave Asian Russia, cross the Urals and live in the European side. He first settled in Tver, but Tver offered few opportunities to make the living he needed in order to put his stepson Pasha through school. Only St Petersburg held out a chance of making a success of his new life. His brother Mikhail had set up a magazine there; he could work in his beloved field of literature if he could only get back home. The problem was getting permission to live there. Although he was permitted to return to European Russia, Moscow and St Petersburg were forbidden him. Once again, he wrote to General Totlebon asking him for just one more favour: get him out of Tver. Five months went by. Then in December 1859, ten years after he left the city in chains, Dostoyevsky was back in St Petersburg.

[1] *Crime and Punishment*, page 15.

[2] Reminiscences of Baron Wrangel, 1854 to 1865, *The Letters of Fyodor Michailovitch Dostoyevsky to his Family and Friends*, page 300.

[3] Letter to General E.I. Totlebon, March 1856, *Ibid*, page 91.

[4] Reminiscences of Baron Wrangel, 1854 to 1865, *Ibid*, page 313.

[5] Reminiscences of D. Grigorovich, 1837 to 1846, *Ibid*, page 265.

[6] *Dostoyevsky: Reminiscences by Anna Dostoyevsky*, page 79.

[7] *The Idiot*, pages 267, 268.

Chapter Eleven
THE TOWER OF BABEL

'They say it is spring in Petersburg. Is it? Still, perhaps it is. Indeed all the signs of spring are there. Half the town is down with 'flu and the other half has at least a cold in the head. These gifts of mother nature fully convince us of her renascence. So it is spring!'[1]

Dostoyevsky loved St Petersburg, and it was to be his home for the rest of his life. In later years he left unwillingly to travel abroad for the sake of his journalism, his second wife and later his health. Under the rule of Alexander II in the late 1850s and early 1860s, St Petersburg was a marginally more relaxed place to live than before Dostoyevsky's imprisonment. Legislation was being prepared that to Dostoyevsky must have seemed an answer to prayer: the Tsar was planning to free the serfs.

The long-awaited liberation happened in 1861. Russia was at last a liberated modern country which had abandoned its feudal ways and joined the modern world — or so many thought. But it was a liberation without land and an emancipation without means. In Russia land ownership has always been less important than land control.

Emancipation liberated the serfs from the personal and individual control of the landowner — no longer could he split up families, force marriages or punish his workers directly — but he still controlled the land, at least for a while. The emancipated serfs were instructed to buy back the land on which they had worked all their lives at terms agreed between the landowner and appointed arbitrators. This left the workers with large mortgages payable in money or services just as when they were serfs. Eventually, of course, they could hope to own and control their land — but the success of the scheme and the prosperity of the liberated serfs depended heavily on the fertility of the land and the type of work required.

Moreover emancipation meant that the landowner was released from any obligation to his workers. Before 1861 he was responsible for the physical and spiritual welfare of the 'souls' who lived on and worked his land and gave back to him its produce. After 1861 he had workers who were independent of him in every way except that they were buying the land. Many ex-serfs found themselves working just as hard as before on the landowner's land, with little time to plough and cultivate the land they were buying to supply their own families and no help or protection from their overlord. It was a compromise emancipation, calculated to keep the landowners pacified, but it lost for ever the support of the workers. Within a few years the system's inadequacies were plain to see and unrest in Russia deepened. In 1881 Tsar Alexander II was assassinated.

The new legislation was welcomed by Dostoyevsky when it came in. It removed the last great barrier between himself and loyalty to the Tsar. It appeared to establish that the Tsarist regime could dispense justice without having to be dismantled. Although, very soon, the inadequacies of the system began to show, the practice of serfdom had in principle been abolished, and Dostoyevsky's loyalty was won.

Just a year after the emancipation, however, in 1862, a series of pamphlets appeared on the streets of St Petersburg urging the population to revolution. 'To the axe!' the pamphlet exhorted, calling on the people to strike at the Imperial Party without restraint in the city squares, in the houses, in the narrow streets.[2] The pamphlets caused Dostoyevsky much distress. They appeared just as a number of fires broke out in St Petersburg with no apparent cause. How the fires started is not known but many people, including Dostoyevsky, attributed them to revolutionary activity. As a reformed revolutionary Dostoyevsky felt obligated to warn others of the error of their ways and so to save them from his fate or worse. There was a great difference, he felt, between getting justice and instigating a revolution: the two were not compatible.

Like many others in St Petersburg he assumed that a well-known radical, Chernyshevsky, was either responsible for the fires or able to influence the perpetrators. Dostoyevsky decided to visit Chernyshevsky to see if he could help stop the fires. Dostoyevsky took a big risk visiting Chernyshevsky. If he had been seen by the authorities he might well have lost his freedom and doomed the magazine *Time* on which he worked. Chernyshevsky recalled Dostoyevsky's visit as somewhat hysterical while Dostoyevsky said he made a calm and considered approach. Whatever the manner of the conversation, Chernyshevsky denied having anything to do with the fires and Dostoyevsky went away reassured. Nevertheless Chernyshevsky was arrested, tried and found guilty of instigating them and, although the evidence was flimsy, he was sent to Siberia.

Dostoyevsky later published a cruel satire depicting a political radical having been swallowed by a crocodile but still spouting his philosophy from inside its stomach. When readers protested, Dostoyevsky denied that he was caricaturing Chernyshevsky, although the piece was so pointed that it was difficult to place any other interpretation on it. Possibly, as an ex-prisoner himself, he realized he should have had more sympathy for his fellow 'unfortunate'. Chernyshevsky did not fare so well as Dostoyevsky: he spent most of the rest of his life in Siberia, only returning to his home town of Saratov to die in 1889.

This incident illustrates the confusion that reigned in Russia after the emancipation of the serfs. Dostoyevsky's mood, like that of many of his contemporaries, went from elation to despair at the situation. His loyalty to the Tsar and Russia's autocratic regime never wavered now, but it soon became obvious that this liberation had not ushered in justice; in fact it compounded the injustices of serfdom. Emancipated serfs were no less bonded to their masters than they had been before. Dostoyevsky was to document mercilessly the effects of poverty on the human psyche. He would observe and explain the motivations of the revolutionary, the atheist, the nihilist and the anarchist in the face of a cruel political regime and an inadequate explanation of God and his justice.

Against this background Mikhail was editing the journal *Time* that he had set up in 1858 just before Dostoyevsky's return. Fyodor, though not permitted to edit any journal, was a contributor to the magazine and, unofficially, had much to do behind the scenes. In addition, he involved himself in many other activities. Having been elected a member of 'The Society for Needy Authors', he immediately arranged a loan from the Society to his fellow prisoner, Durov, now dying in Odessa. He flung himself enthusiastically into a fund-raising event, a performance of Gogol's *The Inspector General*, playing his part as the postmaster with gusto, despite the fact that another member of the cast was Turgenev. He supported the Sunday-school movement, which had initial government backing until it was thought that the schools were being used as a method of subversive education. These endeavours involved Dostoyevsky in the fight for justice without involving him in actual revolutionary movements. He had not lost his keen desire to see human beings better treated but he worked now within the framework of legality.

Most of the time he was preoccupied with his and Mikhail's journal *Time*. The magazine was feeling its way towards a more conservative position than that taken by their competitor, *The Contemporary*. The two magazines represented and polarized the two strands of thought beginning to dominate the Russian political debate. *Time* lauded Russia as it was. It was loyal to the regime and recommended only change that was endorsed by that regime. It saw its role as revealing to Russians the injustices that still existed in their country and the pride they could take in the progress they had already made. It began to take on a particularly nationalistic stance, a tendency that Dostoyevsky was to develop into a creed of his own in his later political writings. By contrast, *The Contemporary*, edited by Nekrasov and contributed to by Turgenev, applauded the westernization of Russia. It advocated the subordination of Russian nationalism to Western values and culture.

Nekrasov initially under-estimated his old friend and rival Dostoyevsky. On the evidence of his first publications after his time in Siberia, Nekrasov stated that Dostoyevsky was finished, but Dostoyevsky had only just begun. He opposed westernization because he felt that the result would be secularization, perhaps an intentional side effect wished for by those who had at one time flirted with atheistic socialism and who saw Orthodox Christianity as an oppressive yoke. Dostoyevsky, now more than ever a believer, did not want to rid Russia of religion for the sake of modernization. He decided to travel to Europe to see for himself how religion fared in the Western world.

He went alone, without Maria. Theirs was now a marriage in name only. Maria hated St Petersburg, and Dostoyevsky's family had never really accepted her. She was aware of this obvious dislike and found that the St Petersburg air aggravated her tuberculosis. So in November 1863 they moved to Moscow where she was looked after by friends and servants, and Dostoyevsky visited her occasionally from St Petersburg. Whenever they were together she bickered with him and accused him of neglect. Maria lived only for attention and Dostoyevsky's mind was on his career. His marriage was a mistake. All his friends and relatives knew it and he did too, within months of marrying Maria, but he never shirked his obligations towards her and her son.

Dostoyevsky saw in Europe all that he dreaded. Shocked at the conditions under which the English poor were forced to live he described London in Dickensian terms. The Crystal Palace, he thought, was a monument to the anti-Christ, the Tower of Babel: 'It is a Biblical sight, something to do with Babylon, some prophecy out of the Apocalypse being fulfilled before your very eyes. You feel that a rich ancient tradition of denial and protest is needed in order not to yield, not to succumb to suppression, not to bow down in worship of fact, and not to idolize Baal.'[3] Western Europe, he perceived, was selling its soul to mammon in the form of science and materialism. When he returned to Russia he wrote about his travels in *Time* under the title 'Winter Notes on Summer Impressions'.

Dostoyevsky's growing xenophobia only emphasized the gulf between himself and Nekrasov and Turgenev of *The Contemporary* who had started him on his career. His new circle included Nikolai Strakhov, an early biographer.

Time was gaining ground in Russian literary circles and re-establishing Dostoyevsky as both a writer of fiction and a journalist, but in 1863 disaster struck. In January of that year rebellion broke out in Poland. The struggle, which was to last a year, would lead to the more aggressive Russification of Polish systems and the tighter rule of Russia over its Polish territory. Russification — the process by which Russian systems of government, bureaucrats, law and control were imposed — provoked a variety of responses and Dostoyevsky felt obliged to make some comment. He commissioned Strakhov to write an article for *Time* on the subject. The article was supposed to toe the government line but somehow Strakhov failed to get the balance right. The censors took offence and the magazine was closed down.

This was indeed a calamity, not only because it took away the platform from which Dostoyevsky was re-establishing his career but because it placed a great financial burden on the brothers. Mikhail had been so confident in the continuing success of the magazine that he had just sold his cigarette factory when the blow struck, leaving him with no means of supporting himself or his family. Fyodor had fewer responsibilities but his epilepsy was growing worse and he wanted to make another trip abroad. The pretext for his last trip had been medicinal, and the change of air had seemed to improve his epilepsy. Moreover one or two medical experts had recommended a second trip, in order to make permission easier to obtain. Now that he was no longer needed at *Time* he re-applied to go abroad, this time with a companion.

Apollinaria Suslova, or Polina, was the second great disaster of Dostoyevsky's love life. A student, she had met him at an evening gathering where he had read excerpts from *The House of the Dead*. Polina was impressed with his dramatic delivery, his voice that shrieked with passion and whispered with tension. But she was a modern woman, a believer in free love, not one to ally herself with just one man.

The affair began passionately and they arranged to go away together. However, Dostoyevsky was not able to travel with her immediately and she went ahead to wait for him in Paris. Unfortunately Dostoyevsky waited too long before he followed her. By the time he reached Paris she had met, fallen in love and gone to bed with one Salvador who swept her off her feet and disappeared just as fast. After his conquest he sent a note saying that he had typhus and that this was probably farewell. This ruse might have worked had Polina not seen him in the street while he was supposed to be dying. When Dostoyevsky arrived in Paris he found a note telling him that it was all over but Polina had not quite gone and he was able to confront her. After a difficult scene during which she threatened to cut Salvador's throat, Dostoyevsky and Polina both calmed down and agreed to travel on together as brother and sister.

The relationship proved difficult to maintain. One problem was that during this trip Dostoyevsky began gambling addictively. The addiction surprised his old friend Baron Wrangel who never saw him gamble in Semipalatinsk although opportunities were plentiful. Nevertheless the casinos of Europe attracted him and like all addicted gamblers he lost hopelessly. Polina spent the rest of the trip lending him money, pawning her jewelry and moving out of hotels under dubious circumstances. In spite of his gambling she stayed with him — until they met the exiled Russian radical, Herzen, and Dostoyevsky passed her off as a near relative. Soon after that Polina went back to Paris to find Salvador.

It would be easy to under-estimate the importance of this relationship in Dostoyevsky's life because of its brevity and failure, but Polina was a firebrand and their mutual attraction was powerful. For years he kept up a correspondence with her that would later make his second wife feel insecure. In the end the correspondence and the friendship faded but it is probable that Polina was the love of his life in spite of the destructive effect they had on each other. He may well have viewed her and their affair with rose-coloured spectacles, however. The relationship was, at best, stormy and neither behaved very honourably towards the other. Polina went on to hold particularly fascist and anti-semitic views.

Dostoyevsky was attracted to fiery personalities but his demands on them suited more compliant women than Polina, and he had yet to approach the kind of woman with whom he could build a successful relationship. He did, however, use the experience in his writing to portray the power of a destructive relationship. The character of Nastasya Filippovna in *The Idiot* is thought to reflect Polina, and the relationship Nastasya suffers with Rogozhin powerfully portrays the effects of a destructive attraction.

After Polina had gone, Dostoyevsky stayed in Europe gambling, until he received word that his wife, Maria, was dying.

[1] Essay I, 'Four Essays', April 13, 1847, *Dostoevsky's Occasional Writings*, page 3.

[2] Hugh Seton-Watson, *The Russian Empire 1801–1917*, page 329.

[3] *Summer Impressions*, page 59.

Chapter Twelve
UNDERGROUND MAN

Maria Dmitryevna Dostoyevskaya rocked herself constantly in the rocking chair at her apartment in Moscow as her husband sat and watched her. Like many in her situation she found it hard, in fact impossible, to face up to her own imminent death. Her conversation avoided the subject. She and Dostoyevsky made plans for the future. They spoke of summer holidays, of getting better, of anything but tuberculosis and death.

When Dostoyevsky suggested that her son, Pasha, should visit her she panicked and accused him of intimating that she was dying. 'She will not see him,' Fyodor wrote to Mikhail. 'You can't blame a consumptive for her state of mind. She has said she will send for him to give him her blessing when she feels she is dying. But she may die this evening, and meanwhile this very morning she was making plans for spending the summer in the country, and removing to Taganrog or Astrakhan in three years' time. It is impossible to remind her about Pasha. She is terribly apprehensive and will take fright at once and say "That means I am very ill, I am dying."'[1]

At times she was lucid; at times she hallucinated. She saw demons in the room and would go into an hysterical rage until the doctor opened the window and shooed the demons out. There was no comfort for her and nothing for Dostoyevsky to do but wait. When she finally took to her bed for the last time, he sat at a desk in her room, listening to her ever shallower breathing and occasional ramblings, staying with her so that he could be with her at the end. While he waited he thought and wrote.

'I'm writing this just for myself, for even if I do address myself to imaginary readers, I do it only because it makes it easier for me to write. It's just a matter of form, nothing else, for as I said before, I'll never have any readers.'[2]

Thus wrote 'underground man', protagonist of the short novel *Notes from the Underground*, written while Maria was dying. In it Dostoyevsky created a type of character which he used again and again in his work: the 'underground man', a generic term he applied to other characters and perhaps his own name for the anti-hero. This was a man of an unredeemed nature. Perhaps he reflected the way Dostoyevsky felt about himself at the time. He, like his protagonist, had failed in love. His marriage had been a disaster. Her life had been shoddy and he had done nothing to improve things for her. Underground man's cynical and harsh tone may have reflected Dostoyevsky's guilt. He was, in a sense, a portrait of guilt and what it does to a human being. Unlike his successor anti-heroes, such as Raskolnikov (*Crime and Punishment*) or even Stavrogin (*The Devils*), there is nothing to like about underground man. In that respect he is more like old Karamazov, father of the brothers Karamazov in the novel of that name, than the almost likeable villains Stavrogin and Raskolnikov.

Underground man takes pride in humiliating other people. Then he feels guilty about it but resents the fact that he is hated because of it. He enters a sado-masochistic cycle of mental torture. If he tries to make things better, he always ends by making them worse. He attends a party at which he is quite clearly not wanted. Once he has forced his way past the protesting but compliant guests, instead of settling quietly down to enjoy himself in their company, he fulfils their worst apprehensions by abusing the guest of honour. The friends make their escape, pursued by underground man, who is desperate to apologize. The friends elude him and he settles for a night with a prostitute whom he proceeds to humiliate by describing to her the ghastliness of her future.

'You're in debt to them, and you'll remain in debt till the end — till the time when the customers refuse to use you. And that's not as far off as you think, for you'd be wrong to rely too much upon your youth. Time moves very fast indeed here. They'll kick you out soon enough.'[3] His mood swings between offering her rescue and humiliating her even further.

Notes from the Underground is a deeply depressing description of the self-destructiveness of the human psyche. In some ways it may have been a catharsis for Dostoyevsky. He knew what it felt like to go to parties where he was not wanted. His fall from grace after the publication of *The Double* had seen him edged out of the top literary cliques, partly because of his own arrogant behaviour. His relationship with his wife was one of guilt-ridden failure. He had pursued her to the altar and then abandoned her, only really returning to attend her death.

As well as the personal significance that underground man may have had for Dostoyevsky as an expiation of his own guilt, he is also the first detailed characterization of that most famous kind of fictional hero, the anti-hero. The term anti-hero is a modern one applied to a kind of character that some believe to be Dostoyevsky's invention. While he may not have been the first ever to use such a character, many of his creations are definitive anti-heroes: major characters with no traditionally heroic qualities. The anti-hero is not a good man but his motivation, characteristics, past and present actions are described with subjective interest. He is often the central character or the pivot around which the story revolves. Raskolnikov, the central character but villain of *Crime and Punishment*, is an obvious anti-hero. Frequently the godly counterparts of such characters suffer by comparison. The power of goodness is difficult to portray because good characters tend not to fight dirty and can appear weak in the face of evil opposition. Just as Hamlet appears weak in the face of his murderous stepfather, so Shatov and Kirilov are little match for Peter Verkhovensky and Stavrogin, the anti-heroes in *The Devils*.

Dostoyevsky had become fascinated by the effects of sin on a man's character. Because he later wanted to write the *Life of a Great Sinner*, he kept letters and notebooks full of plots, stories and descriptions of such a man. The great sin he depicted in *The Devils* was sexual abuse of a little girl much like his childhood friend who died in the hospital grounds after being raped. How does a man live with a crime like that on his conscience? What does it do to him? Why did he do it? Can he be saved?

Dostoyevsky raised and dealt with such questions through his anti-heroes: Raskolnikov in *Crime and Punishment* who murdered two women because they were nasty and he needed their money; Stavrogin in *The Devils* who seduced a child; Smerdyakov in *The Brothers Karamazov* who killed old Karamazov, and Dmitry who suffered for that crime even though he did not do it. Through the eyes of criminals he threw light on human evil, an evil he had discovered in prison and it was an evil that he became an expert at portraying.

But a preoccupation with the darker side of human nature did not entirely dominate Dostoyevsky's time at Maria's bedside. Once again he turned to the New Testament, perhaps in the depths of the night when every breath that Maria fought for pained him as much as it did her. Reading the Bible, he became convinced of the desperate selfishness of putting the 'I' first. In the commandment 'Love thy neighbour as thyself' he saw that submitting the self to other people was necessary to mankind.

He wrote some of what he thought in his notebook, as he waited for Maria's death. 'To love your neighbour as yourself, according to Christ's commandment, is impossible. The law of personality on earth prevents it. The *I* prevents it. [And yet] Christ alone was able to do it, but Christ is eternal, an eternal ideal toward which man aspires and is bound to aspire according to nature's law. And yet after Christ's appearance *as an ideal man in the flesh* it became as clear as daylight that the highest and last development of personality must (at the very end of its development, at the very point of achieving its goal) reach the point at which men will find out, realize and become convinced, utterly convinced, that the greatest use a man can make of his personality, of the fullest development of his *I*, is in one way or another to destroy this *I* to give himself up wholly to all and everyone, selflessly and wholeheartedly. And that is the greatest happiness.'[4]

From the time of Maria's final illness Dostoyevsky felt that selflessness held the secret of salvation. As he watched his wife dying, however, he knew that to destroy the self would make sense only if there was an afterlife. If there was no future life then the only reasonable approach would be to live entirely for one's own gratification, because nothing in the future would compensate for self-sacrifice. Christ's commandment, then, pointed to life after death.

Underground man was a selfish man with a great self-love. In the context of belief, then, he was a sinner. Other Dostoyevsky characters would represent the purity of self sacrifice, as Sonya does in *Crime and Punishment*: she becomes a prostitute, sacrificing her worldly reputation and purity to feed the family who loves her. Such a sacrifice would be meaningless without immortality. By contrast Stavrogin in *The Devils* demonstrates the logical consequence of the failure to believe in immortality: perhaps Dostoyevsky's greatest sinner, he is given over to the flesh and the desires of self.

His last novel, *The Brothers Karamazov*, expresses this idea most succinctly when Miusov quotes Ivan Karamazov: 'But that is not all: he wound up with the assertion that for every individual, like myself, for instance, who does not believe in God or in his own immortality, the moral laws of nature must at once be changed into the exact opposite of the former religious laws, and that self-interest, even if it were to lead to crime, must not only be permitted but even recognized as the necessary, the most rational, and practically the most honourable motive for a man in his position.'[5]

While Fyodor Dostoyevsky was sitting at his wife's bedside, Mikhail had got permission to publish another journal to replace the now defunct *Time*. The new journal, whose first issue was published in March 1864, was called *Epoch*. Mikhail sent a copy to Fyodor to read and evaluate. His first response was not encouraging; he felt that there was still much work to be done. 'Here is my impression,' he wrote; 'the production might have been rather more elegant, the misprints are so numerous that it amounts to slovenliness.' Fyodor did not appreciate the work the censors did on his own contribution, the first part of *Notes from the Underground*: 'Those brutes of censors. Where I made a mock of everything and sometimes blasphemed *for form's sake*, that is passed, but where I deduced from all this the necessity of faith and of Christ — that is suppressed. Are the censors in a plot against the government or something?'[6]

The new journal had to be very careful not to offend the censors: Mikhail had sunk all he had into its production and, since he had sold his cigarette factory, the magazine was his only chance to make a living. Unfortunately, it was proving extremely difficult to guess what would please or offend the censors. The article that had brought down *Time* had been the victim of an unfavourable interpretation. Suspicious minded censors had read into the piece something that the publishers had not intended to say, and they were not given the benefit of the doubt. Consequently *Epoch* was desperate not to publish anything that might be misinterpreted.

However, they paid a price for their careful publishing, for many readers of the old *Time* felt that *Epoch* blunted its effectiveness by compromising too far. Whereas *Time* had had a good following of regular subscribers, few of its old readers remained faithful to *Epoch*. *The Contemporary*, *Time*'s old rival, was back in the marketplace after having been banned for nine months and, with the combined talents of Nekrasov and Turgenev backing the journal, it attracted much more attention and many more readers than *Epoch*.

Turgenev wrote a piece for *Epoch*, even though his main outlet was *The Contemporary*. This did not mean that the rift between him and Dostoyevsky was in any way narrower. (It did not help that payment for Turgenev's piece was long delayed.) Political and religious differences, reflected in their respective journals, aggravated their relationship. They were also divided artistically: Dostoyevsky believed that art was a worthwhile pursuit for its own sake, that writing could involve fantasy, depictions of beauty and the unreal without damaging its function as art, whereas Nekrasov and Turgenev still represented the view that art must have some function beyond just being art, that it must be subordinated to higher social causes such as socialism or westernization. They no longer argued the point as they once did. The different writers simply got on with their individual work and thus represented their different approaches to the public through their journals and books.

However, to say that Dostoyevsky did not want to express any message through his work would be inaccurate. He did not want to represent the world exactly as people experience it but to externalize his characters' personal and moral battles through fantasy, dream sequences and supernatural occurrences. For example in *The Brothers Karamazov* Ivan is visited by the devil who makes predictions about his future. Ivan is an agnostic, so this visitation put him in an awkward position. The devil could be a figment of his imagination, a dream, an hallucination or the real thing. Whatever the explanation, the predictions come true.

Was the devil then real, or was he a device, a parable or a dream? Dostoyevsky felt that the reality of the human psyche could sometimes be better explained by the use of metaphor and fantasy. Moreover he was by this time convinced of the existence of a greater reality. He was not an atheist. His work did not have to be rooted in the world of social realism. In a novel, too close a link with the social realities of the time could mean that the work was limited in its appeal because a detailed knowledge of its realistic background was required. Dostoyevsky had always maintained that art should not serve social or political aims. He regarded metaphor and fantasy as a form of universal language. The idea of the devil, for instance, the evil one, a bogey man, could be understood by almost all cultures without a social explanation. Dostoyevsky wrote his books not just to entertain or make a living. Like Turgenev and his other contemporaries he had something to say through his work, even though his chosen form was sometimes metaphor not realism.

His last novel, *The Brothers Karamazov*, the culmination of various ideas and aspects of faith that he had been attempting to express throughout his writing career since leaving prison, has been cited as one of the greatest Christian apologetics ever written. Dostoyevsky's letters to friends and relatives are full of half-formed ideas and plots. One such novel that never got written, to be called *Atheism*, was to depict a man who journeys through sin and other religions to conversion to Orthodox Christianity. In *Crime and Punishment* the murderer, Raskolnikov, comes to some sort of redemption, and in the novel *The Idiot* Dostoyevsky made a concerted effort to portray a good man, a modern Russian Christ.

Therefore to say that Dostoyevsky believed that art should never be used to promote certain beliefs is not to say that he had no purpose in writing or that he had no message — social, political or religious — that he wanted to communicate. Nevertheless, what he believed and the way he wanted to put it over set him at odds with Turgenev and Nekrasov, and this was to leave him without sufficient outlets for his work. His enmity with these two men was to limit his opportunities for publication in the future.

In April 1864 Maria Dostoyevskaya died. Her death represented one of Dostoyevsky's great failures: he had failed to make a good marriage with her and so had failed to make a good death for her. With sadness Dostoyevsky kept vigil at her bedside and when she died he reflected on the nature of their love. To his old friend Baron Wrangel he wrote: 'I will tell you everything when we meet, but now I will only say that although (because of her strange, mistrustful and morbidly fanciful nature) we were decidedly unhappy together, we could not cease to love each other . . . I had no idea how empty and aching my life would be when the earth was strewn on her coffin.'[7]

Dostoyevsky packed up his notebook jottings and short novel *Underground Man* and left Moscow for St Petersburg to try to make a go of the new journal *Epoch*. This, however, was not to be.

While Fyodor had travelled Europe and waited at his wife's bedside, Mikhail had worked hard to get *Epoch* off the ground. It had taken him a long time to persuade the authorities to let him publish. Consequently the journal was launched too late in the literary season to attract many readers. It was late spring by the time it came out, well after the competition had attracted the readership; and *Epoch*'s establishment view did not impress readers of the old *Time* magazine. Dostoyevsky, although still famous, was not the great draw to readers that Turgenev was. *Epoch* went to press carrying heavy debts and it was mocked by the other magazines.

The strain told on Mikhail. Despite early indications of illness, he was desperate with worry and the need to make money and so he worked until he dropped. Three days after having been rushed home he was diagnosed as suffering from a liver infection. Mikhail died on 10 July 1864.

This was a devastating blow to Fyodor. He had lost his most faithful friend and brother as well as a business partner and supporter. His death not only left Dostoyevsky bereft, it also loaded him with a whole new set of responsibilities. Mikhail had to use the capital from the cigarette factory to live on and to start the new journal. Not only had the money all gone; it had not been enough. *Epoch* was deeply in debt. Dostoyevsky could not officially edit it, nor could he make enough money from it to service the debts and satisfy his own needs, and yet Mikhail's family assumed that Fyodor would now be responsible for them and would take on Mikhail's debts as well as his own. This he did, but it was a heavy burden for he had also committed himself to supporting Pasha, Maria's son.

In the first few days after his brother's death he could choose either to continue to publish *Epoch* or to wind it up and assign it to creditors. He tried, for a few days, to continue publishing it. In making that decision he took on all the magazine's business debts as his own. 'What a pity I did not decide on the first', he wrote to Baron Wrangel,[8] for in the end he had no choice but to cut his losses and assign *Epoch* to creditors. It was better to concentrate on his own work and hope that he could finance everybody through his writing. He needed to find a publisher and to develop a novel that would bail them all out. In the middle of all this his thoughts turned to remarriage.

[1] Letter to Mikhail, March 1864, *Dostoyevsky: A Self Portrait*, page 125.

[2] *Notes from the Underground*, page 122.

[3] *Ibid*, page 176.

[4] *Notebook Jottings: Dostoevsky's Occasional Writings*, footnote, pages 305, 306.

[5] The Brothers Karamazov, page 77.

[6] Letter to Mikhail, March 1864, *Dostoyevsky: A Self Portrait*, page 124.

[7] Letter to Baron Wrangel, March 1865, *Dostoyevsky: A Self Portrait*, page 131.

[8] *Ibid*, page 132.

Chapter Thirteen
THE RAISING OF RASKOLNIKOV

In the months following the deaths of both his wife and Mikhail, Dostoyevsky urgently needed companionship. Maria's death was more a reproach than a bereavement but the loss of Mikhail was devastating. Without his friend, confidant, brother and business partner Dostoyevsky had to struggle to rebuild his life alone. It must have seemed a bitter blow to survive Siberia only to lose Mikhail after such a short time. It was also hard to face the complete failure of their dreams for literary fame, sidetracked by their army career but now beginning to be realized. The only monument to Mikhail's life was a needy family and a mountain of debts, and Fyodor had pledged to take all this on.

Dostoyevsky had no one he could depend on. He sought female companionship but, as ever, his choices and attractions did little to provide him with a more stable environment. Martha Brown was a young woman with a wayward life-style who had travelled extensively in Europe and had lived with various men. When she came back to Russia Dostoyevsky gave her some work on *Epoch* and may have asked her to live with him. Her free manner and liberated behaviour attracted him but she felt that he was not the right partner for her. They wrote to each other for a time until she married an American sailor.

Friendships such as this could not help him solve the difficulties of his day-to-day life. Unstable relationships were far more likely to hinder his progress than to help.

A far more serious relationship developed between Dostoyevsky and Anna Krukovskaya, who later distinguished herself as an active member of the Paris Commune. (This was an attempt by radical French during the Franco-Prussian war to institute a form of communism in France, by turning the recently besieged city of Paris into a commune.) Anna, like so many women who became involved with Dostoyevsky, was deeply moved by him but was probably more fascinated by him than in love with him. She was impressed by his character, his fame and his misfortune.

Anna had sent some stories to Dostoyevsky which he published and paid her for. They entered into a correspondence until her father discovered that she had accepted money for the stories. Anna won her father over to a continued, if censored, correspondence, and she was eager to meet this both famous and infamous writer. Her parents did not view such a prospect with equanimity. Dostoyevsky was a man of limited and uncertain means. He was twice as old as Anna, an epileptic and an ex-convict. An involvement with such a man did not bode well for the future of their daughter.

Anna was a persuasive woman and her parents finally agreed to a chaperoned meeting, probably thinking that this would do less harm than an illicit correspondence. Anna's mother was present at this first exchange, which was not a success. Dostoyevsky was irritated by the older woman's presence and as a result was rude and discourteous. He spoke only in monosyllables and made no attempt to hide his annoyance about being chaperoned. When the agonizingly embarrassing meeting was over, Anna ran to her room screaming at her parents, 'You always spoil everything!'[1]

Dostoyevsky, however, was not to be beaten as easily as that. The next time he and Anna met he contrived to make an unscheduled call, when everyone except Anna and her younger sister Sophia happened to be out. Although the meeting was discovered, the two sisters and Dostoyevsky were in such good spirits that the girls' parents invited him to lunch.

For their daughters' sake the senior Krukovskys did their best to welcome Dostoyevsky into their home but his behaviour left them anxious and perplexed. At one dinner party he began to describe, in detail, the seduction of a young girl by one of his heroes. In the middle of his recital Mrs Krukovskaya cut in, 'Fyodor Michailovitch! For pity's sake, the children are listening!'[2] Sophia, who was more deeply infatuated with Dostoyevsky than was Anna, later said that her mother need not have worried — she had no idea what Dostoyevsky was talking about.

According to Sophia, Dostoyevsky was preoccupied with her sister. He wanted only to speak to her and came to their house for that reason alone. Anna's parents noticed his intensity. At a dinner party Mrs Krukovskaya, once again, felt obliged to rebuke him, this time for monopolizing her daughter and keeping her away from all the other guests. Anna's mother need not have worried that her daughter was spending her affections on an unsuitable partner: Anna herself soon realized that their relationship could not lead to any serious commitment. They simply were not compatible.

Anna was an independent woman, a believer in women's rights and not eager to assume the traditional role of the wife. Dostoyevsky's view of the role of women was more conservative, even though so far he had been attracted to few women who would willingly have conformed to that role. What he needed was constant security in a relationship, someone to keep him steady and to subordinate herself to his requirements. A passionate love affair or a stormy marriage would do nothing for his career and lifestyle. He and Anna argued constantly.

Once again Dostoyevsky was more in love than he was loved, and their relationship bickered its way into exhaustion. The couple continued to write to each other for a while and renewed their friendship in the late 1870s, after Anna's escape from the Paris Commune and not long before Dostoyevsky's death.

Anna was not the only woman Dostoyevsky was courting at that time. In the summer of 1866 he went to his sister's country estate at Lyublino to try to complete *Crime and Punishment*, already being serialized in *The Russian Messenger*. While there he met Elena Pavlovna, a married woman whose husband was dying. Closer to Dostoyevsky in age than was Anna, she was much more willing to subordinate herself to his demanding nature. However she was not, as yet, free to marry. She and Dostoyevsky agreed that once her husband died they would marry, but before that happened Dostoyevsky fell in love with someone else. He later wrote to the wife he chose, Anna Snitkina, 'Elena Pavlovna has taken it all pretty well, and only said to me, "I am very glad I did not consent in the summer or say anything definite, or I should have been shattered." I am very glad she has taken it like this, and I am *now quite* reassured on that score.'[3]

The romance with Anna Snitkina began because of Dostoyevsky's failure to control his business interests properly. Apart from writing *Crime and Punishment* Dostoyevsky had already committed himself to write another novel which he had to submit by November 1866 to another publisher, Stellovsky. Desperate for money, and not blessed with a good head for business, Dostoyevsky had agreed to deliver the manuscript of *The Gambler* on this tight deadline for a ridiculously small amount of money. Not only that, he had agreed to pay a penalty should he fail to deliver by the deadline: he would hand over the publishing rights of all his works to Stellovsky for the next nine years. As the November deadline grew closer it looked more and more likely that Dostoyevsky would lose his only livelihood to an unscrupulous man.

Dostoyevsky was in despair. With four weeks to go he did not believe it was physically possible for him to write a novel. Friends offered to write a chapter apiece if he would set out the plot and plans but he was both too honourable and too proud to let them do that. Another friend, Milyukov, suggested that he dictate his work to a stenographer. Dostoyevsky was doubtful but he had little choice, so he agreed. Milyukov approached a stenography tutor, Pavel Olkhin, and asked him to provide Dostoyevsky with his best student. This turned out to be Anna Snitkina, aged twenty. When Olkhin told her that he had recommended her to Dostoyevsky for the task she was flattered but not convinced that she was up to the job. Her father, who had died not long before, had been a great admirer of Dostoyevsky's writing. Anna and her family had all read his books.

For Anna, the prospect of working for this great writer was both exciting and daunting, and the night before she was due to meet him she could not sleep. But she was ambitious to earn her own way in the world and this was a good opportunity for a serious-minded young person to get experience, contacts and a reputation as a reliable and accurate stenographer. Things were not to turn out quite as she had envisaged during her training.

The independent career that she so coveted was not to be, but the ambition and competence that fuelled her young aspirations were to stand her in good stead in the years to come.

'To tell the truth,' she wrote of their first meeting, 'at first sight I did not at all take to him.'[4] As soon as she introduced herself he forgot her name, and she noticed that his eyes did not match: one pupil was constantly dilated, the result of a seizure. He was just as nervous as she was and completely unused to dictation. He launched into a speedy delivery of a test piece and she could not keep up. When she read it back he thoroughly scolded her for missing a full stop. The only positive comment he made was that he was glad that she was not a man, as men tended to drink. That night she returned promptly at eight with a neat and perfectly worded version of the morning's dictation. Dostoyevsky began to relax.

Once the initial awe and awkwardness of their first meeting wore off they began working well together. Anna Snitkina, like so many women before her, found herself feeling sympathy for the rather sad man she worked with. 'For the first time in my life I had seen a man unhappy, deserted and badly treated, and a feeling of deep compassion and sympathy was born in my heart.'[5]

Feelings deepened in both of them. Five days before they were due to meet their deadline and so stop their working partnership Dostoyevsky confessed that he would miss her and said he would like to see her again. Anna arranged for him to come to tea and meet her socially in the presence of her family, but she was afraid of the kind of impression her family might make on him. They were not rich: her father had been an administrator in the Tsar's palaces and the family owned a few pieces of land on which stood some houses, but these were mortgaged. An added complication for the contemplated afternoon tea was that a friend insisted to Anna that she too should come to tea to meet Dostoyevsky. Anna felt forced to lie to the girl. 'But how to get rid of her, seeing she had invited herself? I thought for a long while and was greatly worried about it; and then I decided on a feminine stratagem: to call her on Thursday morning and to tell her that Dostoevsky had paid us a visit the previous night, on Wednesday, and so was not coming Thursday. That little lie was disgusting to me; but what could I do if I feared her rivalry so much?'[6]

While the couple were falling in love they were also completing their assignment. The day came when the manuscript was complete and ready to deliver, on time, to the publisher. Stellovsky, probably anticipating a last rally on the part of Dostoyevsky, had left the country and so was not available to receive the manuscript. Moreover his offices were closed. After a desperate search for someone to take it they finally persuaded an Inspector of the Police to accept it on Stellovsky's behalf and to give Dostoyevsky a receipt for it as proof of delivery. By then it was ten o'clock at night: they had found a legal recipient just two hours from the deadline. In a celebratory mood the couple went off for a cup of coffee.

Anna was eager to partake in this small victory celebration but she was also worried that accepting a cup of coffee from Dostoyevsky might not be proper. She did not want to get a loose reputation. Moreover she had some feminist opinions: 'As a girl of the sixties, I had a prejudice against all such marks of attention, as the kissing of a woman's hands, or the putting of an arm round her waist in helping her to get out of a cab.'[7] Consequently when he tried to help her out of the cab she informed him promptly that she was all right and would not fall out. Unabashed he replied that he would be delighted if she did, for then he could catch her and hold her.

A few days later, Fyodor proposed to Anna. He did not go down on one knee and ask her to marry him but presented his proposal in the form of a story. He said he wanted her advice on the plot of a new novel. A young woman called Anna (and to begin with Anna Snitkina thought he meant Anna Korvin Krukovskaya) is less than half the age of the man who wants to marry her. Would such a marriage be right? The man, in this case, is worried about the age gap, the sacrifices the young Anna would have to make in her career and life. Anna assured him that the sacrifice would be nothing if she loved him and that the girl would mature quickly. As the story progressed, she gradually realized that he was proposing to her, and she accepted. 'Dostoyevsky's face expressed so much agitation, such anguish of heart that I at last understood that it was not simply a literary discussion, and that I should be dealing a death-blow to his pride and *amour-propre* if I gave an evasive answer. I glanced at his agitated face, so dear to me, and said "I should answer that I love you and shall love you all my life.'"[8]

They were married in February 1867 in St Petersburg's Trinity Cathedral. This ceremony was a far cry from the shabby wedding to Maria in the outpost town of Kuznetsk in 1857. However, history was to repeat itself in at least one aspect of their honeymoon. As a result of drinking too much champagne, Dostoyevsky had two epileptic fits. Consequently Anna, like Maria before her, had to face the terror of his illness very early in their marriage. Unlike Maria she soon came to terms with it and was even able to see the funny side of it. 'This time he did not come round for a rather long time, and when he began to do so — however bitterly and painfully I felt, I had a desire to laugh, for any words he uttered were spoken in German. He said: "Was? Was doch? Lassen Sie micht," and went on with a long string of German phrases.'[9]

Anna Snitkina had married an ex-convict twice her age who suffered from an incurable condition. He had an unreliable and demanding stepson and a mountain of debts. However, he had also just become, if not rich, extremely famous. *Crime and Punishment* was the first of his four great novels to be published and, after he had spent over fifteen years in the literary wilderness, it was to re-establish him as a major literary figure. Typically, though, it was also to create some controversy. It did not receive rave reviews. If anything, it was greeted with anger. Like Dickens, Dostoyevsky had portrayed the conditions of the poor. He brought to lurid life the agonies of poverty in the slums of St Petersburg. In this respect his use of realism was merciless: drunkards, beggars, women dying of consumption and children — dirty, ragged and beaten — stalked the streets of the city amidst the dust and crime of an oppressive Petersburg summer and through this dismal landscape walked the haggard figure of Raskolnikov.

Raskolnikov was a student who had fallen on hard times. He had enough education to grasp the ideas and philosophies of a form of contemporary socialism, spiced with anarchy and nihilism. His was an atheistic view of the world and, as a natural consequence, he lived for self and for the exercise of his own free will. Raskolnikov's decision-making made no reference to a higher moral authority. If God did not exist then humanity was earthbound, like 'underground man', and decisions about life and death had to be made on utilitarian grounds. In a letter of 1878 to N. L. Osmidov, with whom he was corresponding over the merits of Christianity, Dostoyevsky clarified the initial ideas that Raskolnikov expressed: 'Now suppose that there is no God, and no personal immortality (personal immortality and God are one and the same — an identical idea). Tell me then: Why am I to live decently and do good, if I die irrevocably here below? If there is no immortality, I need but live out my appointed day and let the rest go hang.'[10]

Dostoyevsky was fascinated, not with men's motivation to do evil, but with their impulse to do good. He was coming to believe that the only motivation to do good must lie in a belief in God. Raskolnikov's crime stemmed from atheism. Raskolnikov wanted to commit a crime, and the way in which he concluded he should kill an old woman was entirely utilitarian. He asked himself, was this old pawnbroker of any use to anyone? The men in the pub who spoke of her condemned her money-grabbing attitudes and implied that the world would be a great deal better in she was put out of the way. Thus Raskolnikov convinced himself that he had a right to kill her and take her money. He needed the money; she was a wicked old woman; what other morality did he need? For a long time Raskolnikov is trapped by his logic into believing that he did the right thing. He sees himself as a Napoleonic figure acting with almost God-like decisiveness. Psychologically his guilt manifests itself in his dreams and fears but logically he clings on hard to his utilitarian reasoning.

Many reviewers said that the first half of the book was brilliant but after that it degenerated into a kind of morbid self-examination. Many more saw it as an insult to the young people of the time; they thought it implied that St Petersburg's young men were so influenced by nihilistic and atheistic ideas that they were all potential murderers. Critics condemned the link Dostoyevsky made between certain radical ideas and the tendency to crime. Throughout his literature however, and particularly from this novel on, he was keen to expose the logical consequences of certain beliefs. But while some reviewers condemned the novel as poorly written and others defended the young people of St Petersburg, the serial sold by the thousands. Among young people Raskolnikov became the James Dean figure of the 1860s, a rebel with an axe. Several young men were so influenced by Raskolnikov that they actually planned similar murders. A similar double murder actually did take place just before publication. This event, though uninfluenced by the novel, focused public attention on it and no doubt helped its sales.

Crime and Punishment was important not only as a description of social conditions and political ideas but as an indication of the place Christianity was beginning to have in Dostoyevsky's work. Although Raskolnikov was a murderer, he was not unredeemed.

Many critics have made much of his name. The *raskol* or 'old believers', were a sect who refused to accept the new liturgy and the few modernizations to the Orthodox faith imposed by Patriarch Nikon in the seventeenth century, seeing such concessions as a compromise with Rome. Raskolnikov seems to have little in common with this strange sect but one theory is that Dostoyevsky saw the behaviour of extremists, be they political or religious, as comparable. A political sect differed from a religious sect only in its beliefs.

He expands on this theme in a later novel, *The Devils*, about a revolutionary group. However, *raskol* may also have had personal significance to Dostoyevsky. Perhaps Raskolnikov represented Dostoyevsky's own 'old beliefs'; he may have been the ultimate realization of what Dostoyevsky believed became of those who held to the socialist and anarchist political systems he had once embraced.

A central scene in *Crime and Punishment* is when Sonya, the prostitute girlfriend of Raskolnikov, reads to him the story of the raising of Lazarus. It introduces the motif of resurrection. Raskolnikov must die to his old beliefs and therefore to his crime and be raised a redeemed man. Perhaps in the same way Dostoyevsky saw his prison experiences as a death to his old way of life and a resurrection to new beliefs.

In this way Dostoyevsky rescues Raskolnikov from the consequences of his belief in humanistic socialism. In later novels Dostoyevsky was not to be so generous to some of his anti-heroes, but Raskolnikov steps back from suicide without really knowing why. Like Shakespeare's Hamlet, he is afraid to take the step of suicide and so end his 'sea of troubles' because, like Hamlet, he fears that the dreams of such a sleep may be terrible. He may have an immortal soul; he may be required to answer for his actions. This is a fear he would not have if he were truly an atheist.

It is Sonya, the woman who loves him and with whom he falls in love, who shows him the path to Christian redemption. Under Sonya's influence he comes to renounce what he has done and, to an extent, what he has believed. Sonya, however, is an unlikely source for the Christian message. She is a prostitute who sells her body in order to support her drunken father's wife and children, who would starve without her money. When Raskolnikov, still unrepentant, comes to her to confess his crime, she reads to him the story of the raising of Lazarus and she persuades him to give himself up to the authorities.

The publisher was nervous about hearing Christian words from a prostitute, and these scenes were not sent to the printer until considerable revision had been done under the eye of the editor Katkov of *The Russian Messenger*. 'I wrote it in a positive inspiration,' wrote Dostoyevsky to his friend Milyukov of the dispute he was having over the scenes. 'But it may be that it's really bad; however, with them it's not a question of the literary value, but of nervousness about the *morality* of it. In this respect I am in the right: the chapter contains nothing immoral, *quite the contrary* indeed; but they're of another opinion, and moreover see traces of *Nihilism* therein.'[11]

The best portrayal of the character of a nihilist had been credited to Turgenev for his character Bazarov in *Fathers and Sons*. Now that same word was applied to Raskolnikov. Dostoyevsky understood the charge, but he wanted to redeem Raskolnikov from nihilism and it was the manner of his redemption that brought him into conflict with his editors.

Dostoyevsky had portrayed so ghastly a murder that the squeamish had had to give up reading the book, but he had not portrayed the murderer as beyond redemption. Raskolnikov, the anti-hero, is a wrongdoer who is likeable and capable of doing good as well as evil. The duality in human nature was one of

Dostoyevsky's major theories which he felt it was impossible for anyone to deny successfully. In life and faith, good and evil are in constant conflict. At his trial Raskolnikov is defended by friends who testify to his good character, his acts of charity and his heroism in rescuing some children from a fire. At the death of the old drunk Marmaledov, Sonya's father, the priest chants a useless ritual while Raskolnikov gives the family money for the funeral.

Raskolnikov's positive side and Dostoyevsky's hope to convert him and so redeem him worried his editors. They felt that the demarcation between good and evil should be clearer. To them it was unbelievable that a character so unsympathetic should convert to Christianity and be willing to serve his penance. It was also unjust for it meant that, despite his sentence to Siberia, Raskolnikov got away with the crime, at least spiritually. They did not understand the idea that Dostoyevsky had begun to see at his dying wife's bedside when he read the commandment 'Love thy neighbour as thyself' — that actions were less important than attitude of mind. Sonya, though a prostitute, could be a holy person because her simple Christianity and humility were more important to her salvation than being able to live a good life. Raskolnikov could be forgiven because he changed his attitudes and lost the pride that had persuaded him to take another human life.

In the end Raskolnikov's conversion is understated. He and Sonya face the prison sentence together, for she follows him to Siberia. In the last scene Raskolnikov is still unsure and asks himself, 'Can her convictions not be mine now?' Dostoyevsky leaves the reader guessing. 'But that is the beginning of a new story — the story of the gradual renewal of a man, the story of his gradual regeneration, of him passing from one world into another, of his initiation into a new unknown life.'[1][2]

[1] Reminiscences of Sophie Kovalesky, 1866, *The Letters of Fyodor Michailovitch Dostoyevsky to his Family and Friends*, page 323.

[2] *Ibid*, page 326.

[3] Letter to A.G. Snitkina, January 1867, *Dostoyevsky: A Self Portrait*, page 150.

[4] *Dostoevsky: Portrayed by His Wife — The Diary and Reminiscences of Mme. Dostoevsky*, page 9.

[5] *Ibid*, page 18.

[6] *Ibid*, pages 35–36.

[7] *Ibid*, page 39.

[8] *Ibid*, page 46.

[9] *Ibid*, pages 112–13.

10. Letter to N.L. Osmidov, February 1878, *The Letters of Fyodor Michailovitch Dostoyevsky to his Family and Friends*, page 234.

11. Letter to A.P. Milyukov, June 1866, *Ibid*, pages 111–12.

12. *Crime and Punishment*, page 493.

Chapter Fourteen
THE GAMBLER

The success of *Crime and Punishment* did little to alleviate the Dostoyevsky's financial problems. The situation was so bad that Anna sold her dowry in order to pay off some of the more urgent debts. For three months Anna lived with her new husband in the bosom of her new family but, like Maria Isayeva before her, she found that her welcome into that family was neither warm nor willing. Dostoyevsky's sister-in-law, Mikhail's widow, and her family feared that this new wife would divert not only Fyodor's attention but his money from the pressing debts he had agreed to take on after Mikhail's death.

Dostoyevsky's stepson Pasha, Maria's son, was already exhibiting many of the faults of his natural father. He was dissolute, selfish and lazy, and he drank too much. Until Dostoyevsky married Anna, Pasha had set his sights on inheriting the copyright to Dostoyevsky's books. Anna's arrival on the scene made inheriting the copyright very unlikely and so Pasha was all the more keen to get what he could from his new parents as quickly as possible. His requests for money became all the more pressing.

Everyone who knew Dostoyevsky must have viewed his second marriage with trepidation. His first marriage had been a failure from the start and now he had married a young woman more than twenty years his junior. Her inexperience and immaturity alone might have been expected to cause the couple problems. Anna also had an uphill struggle before her in order to convince her critics that she could make a success of her marriage to Dostoyevsky. She had to fight hard to win the support of her new relatives and friends.

It was a struggle in which, at first, she failed. The family hardly acknowledged her presence. They ignored her on the pretext of assuming that she would prefer to be with people her own age, not with her new family. Her new relatives found fault with her housekeeping. When upset, she looked to Dostoyevsky to defend her. He did not do so. His failure in this respect was not so much because he agreed with the criticism of her housekeeping as because it did not matter to him whether it was done well or not. It was all considerably better than a Siberian barracks, after all.

Anna, however, felt let down. Pasha ate them out of house and home, and often sent the maid on false errands in order to raid the larder while she was gone. After three months Anna collapsed in tears and begged Dostoyevsky to take her away from the household. She felt that they must have some time on their own together to get used to being married. Dostoyevsky agreed. With the proceeds of her dowry they paid off their most immediate debts. Then, leaving their things in the care of the remaining family, they left Russia for Europe, intending to stay only three months.

Their sojourn abroad lengthened into almost four years. Their first weeks together were fraught with difficulties and disappointment. Anna is often criticized for keeping diaries that dealt with the petty day-to day existence of their life together, rather than with her observations of the genius at work. She talked about money problems, housekeeping difficulties and small arguments with Dostoyevsky. She also kept an account of his illness.

Biographers and enthusiasts may want to read of Dostoyevsky's struggle to write, of the ideas he may have discussed with her, of the agonies of creating a great work and the anecdotes associated with the artist. Anna, however, was a practical woman and, although she admired her husband's talents and knew very well how exceptional he was as a writer, she admitted in her diary that she could not really understand his work. 'Fiodor thought highly of me, and attributed to me a much deeper understanding of his works than, I think, was actually the case. He was convinced, for instance, that I understood the philosophical side of his novels.'[1] Understanding his thought processes was far less important to Anna than trying to provide the environment in which Dostoyevsky could work.

111

The debts that overshadowed them preoccupied her constantly, and this was reflected in her diaries. When they returned to Russia after their European trip, she took over Dostoyevsky's business arrangements and managed his financial affairs successfully. Even so, he was never out of debt until the year he died. Dostoyevsky did not make it easier for them to save their money or use it to pay off their debts. In their early married life, whatever money he earned he gambled away. His gambling, in fact, dominated their tour of Europe. Anna wrote: 'I was not so much annoyed by his loss, as by the fact that he simply couldn't rid his mind of the idea that he was going to become rich through playing roulette. It is this idea that makes me wild, for it has done us so much harm.'[2]

Dostoyevsky was quite sure that if he only remained calm and kept to one system he would inevitably win at roulette. However, even if his theory was workable he could never keep cool enough to carry it out and he could never quit while he was ahead. He watched more than one fortune pass through his fingers, making him first a rich man and then a pauper, in the same night. Anna paid much of the price for this devastating habit.

In Dresden she went each day for five days to the station to greet her husband on his return from Hamburg where he had gone to gamble. Each day, after finding that he was not on the train, she went to the post office to receive letters begging her to send more money, so that he could pay his way out of the hotel, or pay for the fare to come back. Each time, he received the money with the best of intentions but lost it in one more attempt to win.

Anna pawned almost everything she had: 'I got out my ear-rings and brooch, and looked at them for a long, long time. It seemed to me I was seeing them for the last time.'[3] She became so shabbily dressed that she did not want to go out and meet people. She often remained in their flat crying. In one town they stayed in, when she wanted to listen to the band in the park, she climbed a hill near the park and listened from there. Only occasionally did he use enough discipline to come out ahead, and then the couple were able to redeem the jewellery, shoes, coats and shawls that they had pawned.

All this led to inevitable quarrels about money and sessions of repentance on Dostoyevsky's part. He was not unaware of the folly of his habit nor of the effect it had on Anna. He wrote to Apollon Maikov from Geneva, after watching four thousand roubles he had just won slip through his fingers. 'The worst thing of all is that my nature is ignoble and too passionate: everywhere and in everything I go to extremes; all my life I have always overstepped the mark.'[4]

Although the remorse was genuine enough the repentance was short-lived. Even when Anna's mother came to stay with them Dostoyevsky left for a gambling destination using a pretext in order to hide the real reason from his mother-in-law. Anna connived in this conspiracy. When Dostoyevsky wrote to her for more money, he advised her to tell her mother that he needed the money to replace a mattress he had spoiled during a fit. The long-suffering Anna supported him on this occasion and others because she felt that he needed to get gambling out of his system, or else he could not write.

The gambling caused them great suffering, but she tolerated it as a necessary evil. What Anna feared more than debt were Dostoyevsky's seizures. The begging letters she received from him when he was on one of his gambling jaunts indicated, at least, that he was well. Each time he returned later than expected she feared for his life. She pictured him lying alone somewhere after a convulsion, perhaps even dead from choking on his false teeth or his tongue. Dostoyevsky was also afraid of that kind of death. His fits were frequent and violent.

In the summer of 1867 he wrote to Apollon Maikov of one particularly bad patch he had gone through: 'My fits had begun to recur every week, and to feel and clearly *recognize* this nervous and *cerebral* disturbance was insupportable. My reason was really becoming disturbed — that is the truth. I could feel this; and the disturbance of my nerves sometimes drove me to moments of frenzy.'[5]

The fits often wiped his memory clean and left him depressed and confused for days, unable to recall people he had met, some of whom he knew quite well. They also left him bad-tempered. Strakhov, Dostoyevsky's one-time friend and biographer, describes one example: 'In Switzerland in my presence he so harassed a waiter that the latter took offence and spoke out, "But surely I am a man!"'[6]

Living abroad did little to improve Dostoyevsky's opinion of foreigners. He was already beginning to nurture the xenophobia that was later to colour his attitudes to almost everything that was not Russian. He had an almost paranoid mistrust of foreigners, once telling Anna that he lost at gambling because the Englishman standing next to him had used such a heavy scent that it put him off. The Swiss, he claimed, were petty and argumentative: 'The bourgeois life is developed in this abject little republic to the *ne plus ultra* in the government and in the whole of Switzerland — factions and ceaseless squabbling, pauperism, terrible mediocrity in everything; the workman here is not worth our worker's little finger . . . What drunkenness, what robbery, what petty dishonesty raised to legality in trade. They have, however, a few good traits, which place them immeasurably above the Germans.'[7] The Italians were noisy, and wherever he went he could never get any decent tea. But the people whom he most venomously despised were Russian expatriates living abroad.

These were westernizers, the people who felt that Russia had so little to offer that it was no longer worth living there. They criticized Russia for being industrially backward. Its agriculture was old-fashioned, they said, and its people lived under a near-feudal system. Moreover Russia's religion, they believed, was now held in contempt by most of its people. One of the most distinguished of their number was Turgenev, who had by now set up home in Baden-Baden.

Since Dostoyevsky was in Baden-Baden, it seemed only good manners to visit Turgenev. Besides, Dostoyevsky owed Turgenev money which he could not yet afford to pay back, so he needed to keep the irascible writer sweet. The visit, however, was not a success. Turgenev's view of Russia could hardly have been more opposed to Dostoyevsky's. 'If Russia were destroyed by an earthquake and vanished from the globe it would mean no less to humanity — it would not even be noticed,' he declared to Dostoyevsky.[8] He went on to say that the Russians were bound to crawl in the dust before the Germans, a comment surely calculated to enrage the patriotic and xenophobic Dostoyevsky.

Turgenev was undeterred and told Dostoyevsky that he intended to write an article against the Russophiles and Slavophiles.

Dostoyevsky retorted that he had better get himself a telescope, and direct it on Russia in order to see more clearly what he was writing about. Scenting victory, Dostoyevsky went in for the kill with a particularly patronizing comment about Turgenev's latest novel, which was drawing bad reviews. 'Really I should never have supposed that all the articles derogatory to your novel could have discomposed you to this extent; by God, the thing's not worth getting so angry about. Come spit upon it all.'[9]

The conversation degenerated into a row. Dostoyevsky insulted the German people; Turgenev defended them by saying that any insult to them was an insult to him, as he had now become one. Dostoyevsky realized that, once again, he had overstepped the mark. He apologized and asked Turgenev for forgiveness. The next day Turgenev returned Dostoyevsky's visit, as manners required, but he came at ten in the morning when he knew full well that Dostoyevsky would not be awake. He left his calling card, but the manner of the visit clearly stated that all conversation between them was over.

Dostoyevsky's ever-growing prejudice did not extend to all aspects of foreign culture. He was impressed with Europe's art and architecture. He and Anna made a special trip to Basel in order to view a painting by Holbein the Younger, *The Dead Christ in the Tomb*. Dostoyevsky, fascinated by the painting, climbed on a chair to get a closer look at it. He became so intensely absorbed in it that Anna, afraid he was going to have a fit, had to pull him away. Anna found the picture repulsive, for it portrays Christ as a corpse, blue at the lips and grey with the onset of decay.

In Dostoyevsky's next novel, *The Idiot*, he said it was a picture that could make a man lose his faith, as it seemed to deny all possibility of resurrection: 'But, strange to say, as one looks at the dead body of this tortured man, one cannot help asking oneself the peculiar and interesting question: if such a corpse (and it must have been just like that) was seen by all His disciples, by His future chief apostles, by the women who followed Him and stood by the cross, by all who believed in Him and worshipped Him, then how could they possibly have believed, as they looked at the corpse, that that martyr would rise again? . . . And if, on the eve of crucifixion, the Master could have seen what He would look like when taken from the cross, would He have mounted the cross and died as He did?'[10] In this painting Dostoyevsky saw the embodiment of doubt. In visual form it portrayed much of what he portrayed through his novels: the sense in which the Christian story was almost impossible to believe.

Dostoyevsky went on from Basel to Geneva where he attended an international peace congress. The gathering was addressed by the Italian hero Garibaldi as well as Bakunin, a Russian radical who had escaped from Siberia to join fellow exiles in the West. Dostoyevsky was not impressed. It reminded him of the utopianist preaching of the Petrashevsky circle. He came away feeling that such humanism offered no solutions.

Amid the gambling, the travelling and the writing Anna became pregnant and in her diaries confesses to episodes of crying when Dostoyevsky left her in this state for yet another gambling trip. Their first child, Sonya, was born in Geneva in March 1868. Dostoyevsky was delighted. At last he had found something that could eclipse the pleasure of winning at roulette. Sonya's birth changed his whole attitude to life. Parenthood, he claimed, is three-quarters of what life is about; nothing else matters beside it.

However, this new and uniting joy was short-lived. When Sonya was barely three months old, she caught pneumonia and died. 'She was beginning to know me and love me,' he wrote in despair to Apollon Maikov, 'and smiled when I went near. When I sang to her in my ridiculous voice, she liked to listen. She did not cry or frown when I kissed her; she stopped crying when I went to her. And now people say to comfort me that I shall have other children. But where is Sonya? Where is that little person for whom, I am bold enough to say, I would accept crucifixion if it meant she would live?'[11] The couple were devastated. They cried night after night for their little Sonya, so much so that their unsympathetic neighbours banged on the wall to shut them up.

They could no longer stay in Geneva, so they moved to Vevey on the other side of the lake. Downhearted though they were, their daily routine continued much as before. Anna went to bed early and Dostoyevsky went to bed late. When he got up he would light the fire and drink a strong cup of coffee. After breakfast he would work until four in the afternoon; then he would go out for a cheap meal somewhere. Anna would dine at home, perhaps feeling that her clothes were not smart enough for public show, as much of her good quality clothing had been pawned. After his meal Dostoyevsky would read the *Moscow News* from cover to cover, walk for half an hour and then return home. Once home he relit the fire, had another cup of coffee and started to work again, while Anna went to bed.

The novel he was now writing was the second of his more celebrated novels, *The Idiot*. He hoped that this would be the novel to pull him out of debt and provide a chance for him and Anna to go back to Russia. However, because he had to ask for money in advance, much of what he earned from his books was spent well before publication and his desperation meant a publisher could drive a hard bargain with him.

In writing *The Idiot* Dostoyevsky wished to depict a thoroughly good man, a Christ-like figure placed in Russian society. He wrote to his favourite niece, Sofia: 'There is only one positively beautiful character in the world — Christ.'[12] Dostoyevsky went on to say that he believed that Don Quixote was the most perfect figure of Christian literature to date. He wanted to create a Russian equivalent, a Russian Christ figure who was a holy fool.

It turned out to be far easier to declare his aim to portray such a character than actually to do it. His notes on the development of *The Idiot* show that he started out with a plot and characterization very different from the final ones. In January 1868 he wrote to Maikov that he had just ripped the whole lot up and started again. After eight versions in note form and several different characterizations he settled on the book he published. After publication, he wrote to Sofia that he had not said even a tenth of what he had intended to say.

The main character, Prince Leo Nikolayevich Myshkin, was originally a far cry from the 'perfectly beautiful man' that he finally became. He began as much more of a dual personality, resembling his successor Stavrogin, of *The Devils*, generally believed to represent 'the great sinner' Dostoyevsky wanted to portray. The original Myshkin suffered from spiritual pride and used self-abasement and humiliation as a way of overcoming his baser instincts.

In the final version Myshkin is naturally humble. So self-abasing is he that he appears to be an idiot, thus raising the question: Is someone who is completely humble really an idiot, or is he just perceived to be so by the standards of the outside world? The final Myshkin bears obvious similarities to Christ. He has been away for some years in a Swiss clinic, where he has befriended and helped a young woman, Marie, who had been seduced and cast out of the community. This story parallels Jesus' attitude to Mary Magdalene. Myshkin also wins the affection of the children of the community for both himself and Marie; his affinity with children echoes Jesus' words: 'Whoever does not receive the kingdom of God like a child shall not enter it'.[13] Physically Myshkin resembles the many portrayals of Christ in Russian icons: 'The owner of the cloak with the hood was also a young man of about twenty-six or twenty-seven, slightly above medium height, with very thick, fair hair, hollow cheeks, and a thin pointed and almost white little beard.'[14] Myshkin is also a virgin, although he is not dedicated to celibacy.

As an outsider, Myshkin causes the kind of upset that might be expected of a visiting God. When he pays a visit to some distant relatives in St Petersburg he talks to the servants and treats them equally. Throughout the book, the company he prefers is unreliable and dubious in its reputation: the publicans and sinners of their day.

Jesus once said that the well do not need a physician.[15] In his relationships, particularly with respect to the two women in his life, Myshkin, like Jesus, devotes himself to those who need healing. Natasya Filippovna is a wild-spirited young woman who was seduced by her guardian while she was still very young. She vacillates between her guilt about that time and her desire to become a new woman. Myshkin is attracted to her because she needs him, because he can do something for her. He can save her from a suicidal marriage to the evil Rogozhin and he can forgive her her past.

But Natasya cannot forgive herself and feels that she would destroy the good in Myshkin if she married him. Because Natasya is unable to forgive herself, she is unable to accept forgiveness from Myshkin. Moreover Myshkin's love is not sufficient for her. She does not want to be loved because he can look after her but because he is in love with her. His love, which is three-quarters pity, lacks lust and fiery passion. It is not the kind of love that persuades a woman to marry; it is not like Sonya's love for Raskolnikov in *Crime and Punishment*.

Myshkin has been called a Russian Hamlet. Both men are taken for idiots, whether their idiocy is real, apparent or feigned. Myshkin is sabotaged by his humility, just as Hamlet is sabotaged by his good conscience: not wanting to take revenge for his father's murder without being sure it is the right thing to do, Hamlet is slow to act. Similarly Myshkin, not wanting to commit a selfish or proud act, decides to go to Natasya who is sick and needs him and not to Aglaya with whom he is in love. Like Christ, Myshkin is not successful in the way that society judges success. He does not save Natasya from marriage to Roghozhin, who murders her, and he finishes up mad himself. In addition, his attempts to save Natasya destroy Aglaya, who marries a Polish count and converts to Roman Catholicism, a fate worse than death as far as Dostoyevsky is concerned. Once again a dichotomy is revealed: Myshkin's unselfishness does not heal or save; it hurts and divides.

Dostoyevsky took what he believed to be an ideal man and placed him in a normal environment. This man was humble and loving, able to subjugate himself to others, the living expression of the commandment 'You shall love your neighbour as yourself.'[16] But a person who lives by that commandment appears to be an idiot, a holy fool. Even his names, Leo (for lion) and Myshkin (mouse-like), indicate the tension between holiness and worldly success. Christ was crucified, hardly a successful ending. Myshkin goes mad. An ideal man, then, does not create an ideal world.

Nor is Myshkin in contact with the real world: he is isolated from the Christian community. A funeral is the first Orthodox Christian rite he attends. Dostoyevsky was later to develop the idea that contact with the Christian community is essential to Christian survival. Myshkin is identified as a Christian only because he is called so by other characters, not because he practices the Orthodox faith.

As a representation of the Christian faith Myshkin is weaker and less effective than Sonya in *Crime and Punishment* but as the representation of the ideal man he exposes the world's standards. Dostoyevsky was groping towards an expression of faith in his novels. *The Idiot* was not a critical success, and Dostoyevsky did not think that it achieved what he had wanted, but it consolidated some of the ideas that he was to develop in his later works.

[1] *Dostoevsky: Portrayed by his Wife — The Diary and Reminiscences of Mme. Dostoevsky*, page 153.

[2] *Ibid*, page 118.

[3] *Ibid*, pages 90–91.

[4] Letter to Apollon Maikov, August 1867, *Dostoyevsky: A Self Portrait*, page 163.

[5] *Ibid*, page 162.

[6] Letter to Leo Tolstoy from Strakhov, November 1883, *Dostoevsky: Portrayed by his Wife — The Diary and Reminiscences of Mme. Dostoevsky*, page 232.

[7] Letter to Apollon Maikov, December/January 1867, *Dostoyevsky: A Self Portrait*, page 168.

[8] Letter to Apollon Maikov, August 1867, *The Letters of Fyodor Michailovitch Dostoyevsky to His Family and Friends*, page 121.

[9] *Ibid*, page 123.

[10] *The Idiot*, page 447.

[11] Letter to Apollon Maikov, May 1868, *Dostoyevsky: A Self Portrait*, page 177.

[12] Letter to Sofia Ivanovna, January 1868, *Dostoyevsky: A Self Portrait*, page 169.

[13] Mark 10:15, Revised Standard Version.

[14] *The Idiot*, page 28.

[15] Mark 2:17, Revised Standard Version.

[16] Leviticus 19:18, Revised Standard Version.

Chapter Fifteen
ATHEISM AND SIN

The success of *The Idiot* was not as great as Dostoyevsky had hoped. He was told by his publishers that it had 'shortcomings'.[1]

'What most people regard as fantastic and lacking in universality, *I* hold to be the inmost essence of the truth,'[2] he complained of his critics. However it was not only the critics but also the reading public who did not like *The Idiot*. It certainly did not make sufficient profit to clear enough debts so that Fyodor and Anna could return to Russia. Dostoyevsky was also losing money on reprints of his existing works because he had no agent in Petersburg to defend his interests.

The situation got so bad at home that Pasha, who had spent all the money he had been sent and wanted more, threatened to go to Katkov, Dostoyevsky's publisher, and ask that Dostoyevsky's advance be given directly to him. Dostoyevsky dreaded the effect that this might have, not only on his own financial prospects but also on Katkov's good will and therefore his chances of publishing with him again. When he heard of the threat, Dostoyevsky wrote to Katkov to ask him not to release the money to Pasha. He also wrote to Maikov, to see if he could find out whether Pasha had carried out his threat. In the end he did not; perhaps he was simply attempting to jolt his stepfather into sending more money back to Russia.

Dostoyevsky knew that Pasha was a parasite but the letters he wrote to him show great understanding and perhaps too much tolerance: 'Remember that you can always count on me. So long as I live, I shall regard you as my dear son. I swore to your mother, the night before she died, that I would never forsake you. When you were still a little child, I used to call you my son. How could I, then, forsake you and forget you?'[3] Dostoyevsky never had been able to resist a hard-luck story.

By 1869 Anna was pregnant again. This time she was much more apprehensive about the confinement. They spent a hot summer in Florence which, to Dostoyevsky, was a city that never slept. The noise from the market outside was so great and continuous that Dostoyevsky could not work. To cap it all, a tarantula crept into their room. A search for it flushed it out, but then it disappeared into the mattress. Fyodor and Anna spent an anxious night wondering where it was, and Dostoyevsky recalled the death of a man in Siberia from a tarantula's bite. The spider was found the next morning and was promptly executed.[4]

By this time a change had taken place in Dostoyevsky's personal life. For reasons never quite established he stopped gambling. In 1868 he claimed that he had had a dream in which his father appeared to him and this provided sufficient motivation for him to stop gambling. Other theories are more mundane: he may have had increasing difficulty gaining access to gambling casinos, for not everywhere in Europe was gambling legal. This time, though, Dostoyevsky wrote to Anna that he had finished with gambling. He had made these promises before but now he kept them.

Dostoyevsky had overcome a personal flaw that was a major contributory factor to his financial problems, but he had not yet started to earn sufficient money from his writing to pay off his debts. He still had a lot of work to do. Dostoyevsky was now writing a novel he called *Atheism*. The idea of this book was to track the progress of an atheist and sinner as he explored various philosophies of religion. His journey would take him through some rather weird practices, including flagellation and mutilation, until finally he came to accept Orthodox Christianity.

Atheism never got written in the original form that Dostoyevsky had planned. The central character, however, continued to grip his imagination. At this point Dostoyevsky began to consolidate his idea of portraying a man who lived with the knowledge of having committed a great sin. As a consequence, the proposed novel *Atheism* moved from a description of a search for faith to a description of the life of a great sinner. He wrote to Apollon

Maikov: 'The fundamental idea, which will run through each of the parts [of the novel], is one that has tormented me, consciously and unconsciously, all my life long: it is the question of the existence of God.'[5] Neither *Atheism* nor *The Life of the Great Sinner* were to be published as books in their own right. The character which Dostoyevsky created for these novels, however, would recur, most particularly in his next novel, *The Devils*, which he was to commence writing during the second half of his stay in Europe.

In 1869 he wrote to his niece Sofia: 'In three months, we shall have been exactly two years abroad. In my opinion it's worse than deportation to Siberia. I mean that quite seriously; I'm not exaggerating.'[6]

What Dostoyevsky saw of Europe not only compounded his xenophobia but brought into being a patriotism that went beyond a simple love of country. He became increasingly attracted to a school of thought that defended Russia and her people against Western European influence, proclaimed Russian nationalism and worked to give the Empire a unique identity. Instead of submitting itself to the vagaries of Western Europe as the westernizers recommended, Russia should proclaim its own identity. It did not need to follow the rest of Europe into an inhuman industrial revolution. If it did so it would lose its national character in a mass of factories. It needed to go back to the roots of its culture and build a country and an empire on traditional Russian values.

Russia, however, was such a huge and diverse country that it was difficult to identify one culture, or even one language, that was common to all its citizens and could identify Russia as a unit. One solution to this problem lay in identifying Russian culture with the Slavic language and culture. In the Middle Ages, when Christianity came to Russia, the language of the Orthodox church was church Slavonic, just as the language of the Roman church was Latin. It began life as a clerical language, but, unlike Latin, Slavonic became the basis for the common form of Russian European speech. Thus when Russians looked for their cultural roots they looked to the church and to the Slavic people.

The Slavs were the indigenous inhabitants of the geographical areas of Bulgaria, Yugoslavia and Montenegro. Not all Slavs were under Russian rule; they were small independent countries. Slavophiles believed that the Slavs should be under Russia because in the Slavic people pulsed the purest form of Russian blood, spirit and culture. Slavophiles therefore supported moves to defend the Slavs from outside enemies such as the Turks, even advocating war against such oppressors in order to liberate the Slavs from foreign rule and bring them under Russian jurisdiction.

Russophiles based their political beliefs on a similarly patriotic philosophy. Rather than see their country's traditions diluted by Western values of materialism, science, industrialization and gradual secularization, Russophiles wanted a united Russia that encouraged the Russian peasant spirit, honoured the Tsar and respected and practised the religion of Orthodoxy.

Both schools of thought were attractive to Dostoyevsky, for they were in line with much of what he already believed. One writer that Dostoyevsky read during his time abroad was Nikolai Danilevsky. Like Dostoyevsky, Danilevsky had been a member of the Petrashevsky circle and a keen advocate of Fourier. Also like Dostoyevsky he had undergone a conservative conversion. His book *Russia and Europe* was serialized in 1869 in a journal called *Dawn*, which Dostoyevsky was sent while he was abroad. This journal, a successor to Dostoyevsky's own journals *Time* and *Epoch*, was edited by his friends Strakhov and Maikov. In *Russia and Europe* Danilevsky attempted to re-establish the doctrine of the Slavophiles. Danilevsky was trained as a natural scientist and his racial philosophy seemed to presage the later use of the theory of evolution to justify racism. A dominant race, he thought, has a right to survive and flourish; a weaker race can justifiably be oppressed.

Danilevsky stated that four different races, Jews, Greeks, Romans and Western Europeans had dominated the world in different areas of human interaction: the Jews in religion, the Greeks in culture, the Romans through politics, and Western Europe through economics. The Slavs and the Russians, he claimed, grew from common racial roots and were irrevocably linked with each other. Europe was their natural enemy and it was now their turn, whether by military force or united spirit, to dominate the world in the areas of religion and culture. The Slavs were at the beginning of their most influential era. Danilevsky regarded their cause as so important that he was willing to tolerate the subordination of ordinary human rights, such as freedom and education, in order to achieve the Slavic ideal. None of these things would be worth anything until Slavdom had received its proper place in human history.

This was the political philosophy that now began to attract Dostoyevsky. He would develop it and link it to Christianity, not so much in his fiction as in his later political writings. In 1869 he wrote to Maikov and suggested that he, Maikov, write a national poem depicting Russia conquering Constantinople and restoring to it its status as the capital of the Christian world. Dostoyevsky, though not a poet, advised his friend on the metre and style of the poem. The latter indicates how firmly Dostoyevsky believed in the theory of Russia as a uniquely Christian nation, with the right even to invade Constantinople in order to resurrect it as the capital of Christendom.

Perhaps because he felt alienated abroad, Dostoyevsky had come to regard Russia in a very rosy light and Europe as its inferior. In his earlier travels, in 1862, Dostoyevsky had condemned London's Crystal Palace as a representation of the Tower of Babel. He now saw industrialization and the advance of science as being closely linked to a loss of faith. European nations, he observed, were becoming secular.

'In Western Europe the peoples have lost Christ (Catholicism is to blame), and therefore Western Europe is tottering to its fall', he said in a letter to Strakhov, in 1871, just before he returned home to Russia.[7] Even the brilliant architecture of the Piazza San Marco, which he admired, could not bring him to concede that Europe had anything superior to offer. He had come to believe that Russia was not only a great nation, but a holy nation. Russia had a better grasp of religious truth than did any other nation. Very soon Dostoyevsky would state that it was Russia's duty to point the way to the rest of the world.

Not surprisingly, Dostoyevsky wanted to visit a Slavic country. In August 1869, just one month before their second baby was due, the couple made a visit to Prague in Czechoslovakia. They had hoped to have the baby there but they were able to stay only

125

three days: none of the apartments in Prague were furnished and it would have cost too much for the couple to arrange furniture for themselves. They gave up and returned to Dresden where, in September, their second daughter was born. Lyubov was a fine healthy child with whom Dostoyevsky fell in love immediately. This time he would not be bereaved. Lyubov would survive not only her childhood but her father and would write an interesting, if sometimes inaccurate, account of her father's life.

[1] Letter to Sofia Ivanovna, March 1869, *The Letters of Fyodor Michailovitch Dostoyevsky to His Family and Friends*, page 170.

[2] Letter to N.N. Strakhov, February/March 1869, *The Letters of Fyodor Michailovitch Dostoyevsky to His Family and Friends*, page 167.

[3] Letter to P.A. Isayev, February/March 1868, *The Letters of Fyodor Michailovitch Dostoyevsky to His Family and Friends*, page 145.

[4] 'Piccola Bestia', *Diary of a Writer*, page 428.

[5] Letter to Apollon Maikov, March/April 1870, *The Letters of Fyodor Michailovitch Dostoyevsky to His Family and Friends*, page 190.

[6] Letter to Sofia Ivanovna, January/February, *The Letters of Fyodor Michailovitch Dostoyevsky to His Family and Friends*, page 161.

[7] Letter to N.N. Strakhov, May 1871, *The Letters of Fyodor Michailovitch Dostoyevsky to His Family and Friends*, page 219.

Chapter Sixteen
THE GADARENE SWINE

'And when he had come out of the boat, there met him out of the tombs a man with an unclean spirit, who had lived among the tombs; and no one could bind him any more, even with a chain; for he had often been bound with fetters and chains, but the chains he wrenched apart, and the fetters he broke in pieces; and no one had the strength to subdue him. Night and day among the tombs and on the mountains he was always crying out, and bruising himself with stones. And when he saw Jesus from afar, he ran and worshipped him; and crying out with a loud voice, he said, "What have you to do with me, Jesus, Son of the Most High God? I adjure you by God, do not torment me." For he had said to him, "Come out of the man, you unclean spirit!" And Jesus asked him, "What is your name?" He replied, "My name is Legion; for we are many." And he begged him eagerly not to send them out of the country. Now a great herd of swine was feeding there on the hillside; and they begged him, "Send us to the swine, let us enter them." So he gave them leave. And the unclean spirits came out, and entered the swine; and the herd, numbering about two thousand, rushed down the steep bank into the sea, and were drowned in the sea.'[1]

In the darkness of a Moscow park a young man call Ivanov was lured by his fellow students to a meeting. He was taken by trickery or violence to a small grotto in the grounds of the Moscow Agricultural College, where five men attacked him and held him down. He screamed for help but the park was deserted. He bit and kicked his attackers but only managed to inflict a small wound on the finger of one of them. There were too many of them for even a strong young man to overcome. They set a gun against the back of his neck and fired. The bullet came out through his eye. Once he was dead, they bound him and flung him into the park lake, where he was later found frozen solid in a block of ice.

A few weeks before, in the autumn of 1869, while the Dostoyevskys were still in Dresden, they had received a visit from Anna's brother, Ivan, a friend of the doomed student Ivanov. Ivan told the couple of the student unrest in the college and of the spread of nihilistic ideas. He spoke of the large number of students fascinated with secret societies and revolution. It must have stirred Dostoyevsky's memory to hear of conspiracies, illicit gatherings and feverish discussions. He felt apprehensive, however, for he knew from personal experience that these conspiracies usually ended in disaster. He was horrified to read, a few weeks later, of the death of his brother-in-law's friend.

Dostoyevsky once wrote that if someone could give him the crime he would create the criminal. The murder of the young student gave him a plot into which to weave his own characterizations. The event inspired his next novel, *The Devils*, sometimes called *The Possessed*. In it Dostoyevsky combined a fictional retelling of the events surrounding the murder with his knowledge of conspiracy and revolution.

Ivanov's murder was an act of terrorism led by a dangerous student revolutionary, Sergei Nechayev. Nechayev had been trained by the well-seasoned revolutionary Mikhail Bakunin, a follower of Hegel's philosophy who, like Dostoyevsky, had served time in Siberia. In the late 1860s Bakunin and Nechayev collaborated on writing a training manual for revolutionaries called *Revolutionary Catechism*. Armed with his catechism, Nechayev set up an organization called 'The People's Justice'. An axe was their mascot and revolution was their aim. The idea was to destabilize the country through terrorist cells of about five men. It was one of these cells that killed Ivanov, and Nechayev himself was its leader.

The group of five terrorists under Nechayev wanted to see the Tsar brought down on the ninth anniversary of the end of serfdom, but Ivan Ivanov's death curtailed their plans. Just why Ivanov was murdered is not known. It is probable that his initial interest in the group was as an intellectual, keen on ideas about change but not so enthusiastic about direct action. Once he knew what the group was about he wanted no part in their activities, but by then he was already too deeply involved. He knew too much. Whether he was killed as an example to others, as a punishment, at the whim of the evil Nechayev, or as a method of ensuring the loyalty of the others is a matter for speculation. Whatever the reason, after the killing the gang was implicated and Nechayev had to leave the country. He was arrested in Zurich in 1872, nearly three years later, and handed back to Russia where he stood trial. He died in the St Peter and Paul Fortress in 1882, having served less than half his sentence.

The incident fired Dostoyevsky's imagination. He had told Maikov and others that he intended to write a novel both about an atheist who found faith and about a man who had committed a great sin. *The Devils* provided him with the opportunity to explore both possibilities. Dostoyevsky's great sinner, his atheist, was a man searching for God and an answer to the external questions. If there is a loving God, why does suffering exist in his world? In what way do we have free will and from where do our moral perceptions originate? In the murderers' revolutionary philosophies Dostoyevsky saw a way of exploring evil, suffering and conflict, while at the same time exposing nihilistic atheism as fraud. To do this he caricatured the main participants in the murder.

Historians have complained that the mix of fact and fiction makes it difficult to separate Dostoyevsky's myth from the truth. But the truth Dostoyevsky sought to expose had only a tenuous link with the murder of Ivan Ivanov. 'I have never known and still do not know anything about either Nechaev or Ivanov, or the circumstances of the murder, except from the newspapers,' he wrote to his publisher. 'And even if I had, I should not have copied them. I use only the accomplished fact. My fancy may be altogether different from what actually happened, and my Peter Verkhovensky completely unlike Nechaev; but I think that . . . my imagination has created the character, the type, that corresponds to this crime.'[2]

While *The Devils* is rooted in reality it is probably the most symbolic of his major works. Dostoyevsky often used representative names: Stavrogin, the great sinner of *The Devils* derives from both *stavros* or 'cross' and *rog* or 'horn'. At other times Dostoyevsky used physical features to suggest themes. Pyotr Verkhovensky, the leader of the terrorist group, was snake-like in appearance: 'His head was elongated at the back and somewhat flattened at the sides, so that his face looked rather sharp. His forehead was high and narrow, but his features rather small; his eyes were sharp, his nose small and pointed, his lips long and thin.'[3] Even the novel's title suggests themes: *The Devils* sometimes called *The Possessed*, is based on the story of the Gadarene swine, as one of the characters explains.

'But now an idea has occurred to me; *une comparaison*. An awful lot of ideas keep occurring to me now. You see, that's just like our Russia. These devils who go out of the sick man and enter the swine — those are all the sores, all the poisonous exhalations, all the impurities, all the big and little devils, that have accumulated in our great and beloved invalid, in our Russia, for centuries! . . . They are we, we and them, and Peter — *et les autres avec lui*, and perhaps I at the head of them all, and we shall cast ourselves down, the raving and the possessed, from the cliff into the sea and shall all be drowned, and serve us right, for that is all we are good for.'[4]

The five terrorists in *The Devils* were possessed with an idea that drove them mad, an idea that had infected Russia: they wished to break down society, create anarchy and replace the old ways with an irreligious socialist utopia dependent on the West. Much of their plotting occurred in a place whose name, Fillipov, recalled a predecessor in revolution: the Russian heretic Danilo Fillipov who, as a monk, decided that Christianity could do away with authority and who flung all the rule books into the river.

Exposing their ideas as mercilessly as he could, Dostoyevsky cast the demons into his characters. They became possessed by their objectives, but everything they attempted to achieve ended only in disaster, taking them ever farther from their goals. Pyotr Verkhovenksy's idea to murder the apparent informer, Shatov, was supposed to rid the group of a threat to their existence and bind them ever more closely together in a loyal conspiracy. It did nothing of the sort. In the course of the chaotic and brutal murder, the group fragmented. Their violent act became the catalyst for their own destruction.

The story of the Gadarene swine is not the only biblical allusion in *The Devils*. Geir Kjetsaa in his biography *Dostoyevsky: A Writer's Life* suggests that the characters of Stavrogin and Pyotr Verkhovensky are based on the first and second beasts of the Apocalypse. Just as Prince Myshkin is a contemporary representation of Christ in human form, so these characters are human representations of beasts in Revelation. Geir Kjetsaa points out that Stavrogin is beast-like; he bites someone's ear, and much of the imagery used to describe him is related to birds of prey. Pyotr, who is snake-like, first appears in a chapter called 'The Wise Serpent'. Like the second beast in Revelation 12, he prepares the way for the first beast, to whom he is devoted but who fails to fulfil his dreams.

Stavrogin is infected by apathy, the mark of the church at Laodicea in Revelation 3. 'And to the angel of the church in Laodicea write: . . . "I know your works: you are neither cold nor hot. Would that you were cold or hot!"'[5] Knowing that his wife is going to be murdered, Stavrogin neither wants it to happen nor tries to stop it and it is the same kind of bored, disinterested curiosity that led him to commit his great sin earlier in his life.

A final chapter, 'Stavrogin's Confession', is often added to current editions of *The Devils* as an appendix. In this chapter, left unpublished in Dostoyevsky's day because Katkov felt it was too indecent to offer to his readers, Stavrogin goes to the priest, Tikhon, and confesses that he seduced a little girl of twelve. The child suffers such shame that she hangs herself but she reappears to Stavrogin in his dreams, shaking her little fist. It is not a pleasant story, and it is all the harder to accept in Stavrogin who, though he is entirely dishonourable, is not as repulsive as his counterpart Pyotr Verkhovensky who confines himself to straightforward murder and political conspiracy. In Stavrogin, the duality in human nature is evident. He attempts to live with the evil within himself. But after his great crime he cannot forgive himself and so he goes to Tikhon with a written confession that he intends to publish as a form of expiation. However, Tikhon discourages this. Publication is, after all, a grand gesture, and an egotistical thing to do. Complete obscurity is preferable, but

Stavrogin is too proud to go through with that. In the end he too hangs himself.

Suicide, murder, futile death are the melodramatic climax of *The Devils*. Just as the Gadarene swine flung themselves into the sea, so the protagonists of the novel die as the result of their own actions. This is as true of Kirilov, the other major suicide in the novel, as Stavrogin, even though the two men die for quite different reasons. Stavrogin cannot forgive himself and so cannot live with himself; Kirilov commits suicide for an idea. His suicide seems to be a utilitarian act: he offers it to the group of five, so that they can pin Shatov's murder on him. But this is not like the death of a kamikaze pilot, even though Kirilov is offering his death to the party: he cares little for the cause, for he wonders what relevance any man's action can have in a meaningless world. Instead, this is an act of individual free will: because he is an atheist and does not believe in immortality, he believes that suicide is the ultimate assertion of his free will.

'For three years I've been searching for the attribute of my divinity, and I've found it: the attribute of my divinity is Self-Will! That's all I can do to prove in the main point my defiance and my new terrible freedom. For it is terrible. I am killing myself to show my defiance and my new terrible freedom.'[6]

Much of the philosophical discussion in *The Devils* is concerned with the existence of God. The characters constantly ask themselves and each other if they believe in God. Are they atheists or believers, and what are the implications of their beliefs? To Stavrogin, Dostoyevsky attributes words similar to those he wrote to Natalya Fonvizina in 1854: 'But didn't you tell me,' Shatov accuses Stavrogin, 'that if it were mathematically proved to you that truth was outside Christ, you would rather remain with Christ than with truth?'[7] This identification with Stavrogin may have been the source of the accusation that Dostoyevsky shared not only Stavrogin's doubts but also his crime.

In a letter from Nikolai Strakhov to Leo Tolstoy (published in 1913 after the deaths of both Strakhov and Dostoyevsky) Strakhov, Dostoyevsky's one-time friend and biographer, makes this accusation. Dostoyevsky's wife roundly rebutted the charges. She rightly pointed out that if Dostoyevsky had had to commit all the crimes he portrayed he would have been not only a rapist but a murderer — and unlikely to have got away with it. In the end, little credence has been given to these accusations.

The discussion about God in *The Devils* reveals the conflict in Dostoyevsky's own faith. He could believe in Christ but found it hard to believe in God. Shatov, the victim, is sometimes thought to be the character who most reflects Dostoyevsky's uncertainty. Even Shatov's name means 'shaky' or 'loose minded'. Shatov bears some other similarities to Dostoyevsky: He was a revolutionary who went away for four years, during which time he was converted to some sort of faith, which makes him a danger to the group. (Like Dostoyevsky, he wants to believe.) When asked whether he believes in God he says, 'I shall believe in God.'[8]

In *The Devils* Dostoyevsky takes revolutionary beliefs and works them out in the characters to logical extremes. Just as Raskolnikov's personal philosophy led him to justify murder as a utilitarian act, so the beliefs of the characters in *The Devils* lead them inexorably to the tragic, but logical, consequences. Unlike *Crime and Punishment*, *The Devils* offers no salvation to the protagonists. It is a portrait of evil, of darkness without redemption. Even the wife and newly born child of Shatov are not allowed to live to carry some kind of torch of hope at the end of the novel.

The only indication of Christian influence in *The Devils* is its setting: a church-going community. Nevertheless, this background has little power in the situation: the authorities are weak. Western liberalism, of the sort that Dostoyevsky himself once embraced, is the dominant philosophical force, and it is the consequences of liberalism that Dostoyevsky examines. The father, Stepan Verkhovensky, holds to the kind of liberalism that Dostoyevsky himself had embraced in the 1840s. Pyotr, his son, as well as being his physical offspring is also the extension of Stepan's beliefs from liberalism to nihilism. As the 'devils' flee or destroy themselves at the end of the novel, Dostoyevsky himself exorcizes a dark ghost. A catharsis occurs in Dostoyevsky's writing which prepares him to portray more of the positive side of life in his final two novels.

DOSTOYEVSKY

[1] Mark 5:2–23, Revised Standard Version.

[2] Letter to M.N. Katkov, October 1870, *Dostoyevsky: A Self Portrait*, pages 192–93.

[3] *The Devils*, page 187.

[4] *Ibid*, pages 647–48.

[5] Revelation 3:14–15, Revised Standard Version.

[6] *The Devils*, page 615.

[7] *Ibid*, page 255.

[8] *Ibid*, page 259.

Chapter Seventeen
DEBTS AND CREDIT

Anna Dostoyevsky sat at a table opposite an angry man, a creditor of her husband's. Her welcome back to Russia was to deal with the queue of such creditors who besieged their apartment. Most creditors had been owed their money for the full four years that the Dostoyevskys had been abroad. Other debts went back to the time of Mikhail's death if not before that, to the collapse of their first journal *Time*.

This creditor proved particularly difficult to shift. Almost past negotiating with, he demanded cash on the table immediately. He told Anna that the debtors' prison was where he intended to put Fyodor Dostoyevsky if the debt was not repaid immediately.

The Dostoyevskys had no money, as Anna well knew, so she brazened the situation out. She told the creditor that if he went to the trouble of throwing Dostoyevsky into prison she would find an apartment near the prison, visit her husband regularly and provide him with food and the means to work. In short, she would make his time in prison so comfortable that the creditor would have only the meagre satisfaction of seeing a man flung in a gaol where he could rest comfortably and thus delay even further the possibility of repaying the debt. The creditor saw that she was serious. There would indeed be no profit for him in immobilizing Dostoyevsky in a debtors' gaol. He backed down and they renegotiated the debt.

Thus began Anna's lifelong career as manager of Dostoyevsky's estate and business affairs. Her ambition to earn her living may not have been fulfilled in quite the way she had intended but her contribution to her husband's career, and particularly the work of building up his reputation that she continued after his death, should never be underestimated.

However, in Petersburg in 1871 there seemed to be a thousand creditors outside the door and thousands of roubles yet to pay. On their return Anna had hoped to clear the debts by selling her small house in Peski, part of her inheritance that she had let during their absence, but the tenant had been unreliable. He had failed to pay his taxes and so the house had been sold at much less than its value, which did not leave nearly enough to pay their debts. Not only that, when they returned they discovered that many of their personal possessions left in the care of the family had been sold in order to cover debts and shortfalls in what Dostoyevsky had sent from abroad. Much furniture and many treasures now had to be replaced. Worst of all, Dostoyevsky's library, including valuable signed first editions, had been broken up and sold by his errant stepson Pasha. Anna commented in her own diary that this was a great loss to them and, although she managed to buy back some of the books, she could never fully replace the rare books that Dostoyevsky had so carefully collected.

The four years of travel had included many significant events: watching her husband gamble away fortunes and pawn her most valued possessions; the birth and death of their first child and the strain and fear of a second pregnancy and birth; coming to terms with her husband's worsening epilepsy and hacking cough; returning home just a week before their third child, Fyodor, or Fedya, was born. After such an eventful time it is small wonder that she was told she had aged: 'My women friends assured me that I had aged terribly during those four years, and reproached me for paying no attention to my appearance, and for not dressing fashionably.'[1]

Life abroad may have been hard on Anna but she felt that it had benefitted Dostoyevsky, although perhaps that was partly due to her influence. She said with some satisfaction on their return: 'There is no doubt that during his retirement from Russia, in his new situation, and as a result of long and quiet reflection, there occurred that particular unfolding of the Christian spirit that had always lived in him. That essential change was evident to all his friends, when Dostoyevsky returned from abroad. He continuously turned the conversation to religious themes.'[2]

Despite his new, easygoing manner with his friends and his increasing interest in Christianity, Dostoyevsky was still easily upset by financial matters. He was enraged when rich Aunt Kumanina died and left forty thousand roubles to a monastery. The strain of carrying not only his own debts but also Mikhail's must have made his aunt's action seem a bitter blow. He respected the church, but he knew it was rich and he was poor. Just as he had badgered his relatives for money from his father's will, he contested his aunt's decision. The ensuing argument was to split the family apart. His sister Vera and his favourite niece, Sofia, stood firm against him. Unlike the other beneficiaries, he had received an advance against his inheritance. By contesting the will he prevented anyone from benefitting at all. Sofia had received many of his letters and he dedicated the first edition of *The Idiot* to her, but in later editions her name was removed. The feud was to carry on until the day of his death.

Dostoyevsky could not master his disappointment. His debts were still pressing and a life of toil and constant financial juggling stretched before him and his family. Anna decided that she should try to get a job as a stenographer. The children were settled at home with the maid, so Anna now had the time to work, but Dostoyevsky, overwhelmed by jealousy, could not tolerate the idea. Despite the fact that Anna even dressed in a dowdy fashion to try to allay his fears, he could not trust her or other men, and she had to give up the idea of going out to work. However, the need to make money was so urgent that Anna decided that the Dostoyevskys should go into publishing themselves.

At that time in Russia most major novels were published first in serial form in one of the literary journals and then in a book edition issued by a printer. Anna saw that the more middlemen there were involved in the process, the less money the Dostoyevskys received from the profits of their books. Anna decided that they must publish *The Devils* themselves.

The Devils had already been serialized by Katkov in *The Russian Messenger*, but Anna saw to it that they kept the rights to publish it in book form. By avoiding a middleman they received less money up front, but once they started selling the books to the booksellers they received payment immediately and much more directly. Anna sold the books from their apartment. Queues of booksellers stood at the door and Anna served each of them personally. The domestic upheaval worried the maid. Hearing people come to the door and ask for *The Devils*, she became convinced that some sort of witchcraft was going on and complained that since Satan had come into the house the poor boy Fedya had not been able to sleep.

Writing *The Devils* temporarily exhausted Dostoyevsky of ideas. He too decided that he must get a job, and by the end of 1872 he was offered a post editing a weekly newspaper published by Prince Meshchersky, a well-intentioned man but very conservative politically. The prince's respectable conservatism persuaded the authorities to restore to Dostoyevsky another of his civil rights: the right to edit a publication. Over the years many of Dostoyevsky's ideas had become more conservative and this enabled Prince Meshchersky to plead successfully on his behalf. Dostoyevsky remained, however, under surveillance by the Third Department, or secret police.

Dostoyevsky accepted the editorship and began to work for Prince Meshchersky. The task was not easy. He found the censors awkward and interfering. They altered his work constantly and sometimes actually prevented him from publishing some parts of the newspaper.

The censors were not the only people to make life as an editor difficult for Dostoyevsky. Dostoyevsky was hired on the understanding that Prince Meshchersky would contribute frequently to the newspaper. This left Dostoyevsky with the delicate job of editing his own employer who according to Dostoyevsky, was 'illiterate to the point of incomprehensibility and with howlers that would have made him a laughing stock — for ten years.'[3] Dostoyevsky himself was so demanding an editor that his colleagues nicknamed him 'spitfire'.

Not only that, although Dostoyevsky had become conservative himself, he did not find all the prince's opinions either to his taste or professionally acceptable. They argued often over what the censors might or might not allow and over what Dostoyevsky thought was permissible. He was enraged by one of Meshchersky's articles that advocated rounding up radical students and putting them in one place, so that they could be watched more easily by the secret police. In the end Dostoyevsky went to gaol because of his employer. The good prince had neglected to ask permission to quote the Tsar in one of his articles. The error was, of course, ultimately the editor's responsibility and Dostoyevsky's punishment was two days in gaol, which the authorities allowed him to serve at his own convenience.

Editing the newspaper also took him away from his family. St Petersburg in the summer was no place for young children to be cooped up in a four-roomed apartment, so the Dostoyevskys rented a small wooden house in Staraya Russa, about a hundred and thirty miles from St Petersburg, for the summer months. Because of his commitment to *The Citizen*, Dostoyevsky could not always join them. He hated being separated from his children and was constantly worried about their welfare. If he did not receive regular correspondence from Anna reassuring him, he became convinced that something dreadful had happened to them. He wrote: 'Once more I beg and implore you: Write about once every five days, if it is only twelve lines, like a telegram, about the children's health and your own. You cannot believe how much I worry about the children and what I suffer on this account. Now, not having received any letters, I can only think of them. If I don't hear something by Tuesday i.e. by the day after tomorrow, I shall send a telegram.'[4]

Despite the numerous disadvantages of editing *The Citizen*, they needed the money and the newspaper gave him an opportunity that he had not had so far. Unable as yet to write another novel, Dostoyevsky concluded that some sort of journal or diary would be the next step in his writing career. *The Citizen* offered him the opportunity to write what became known as the *Diary of a Writer*, which at first appeared as a newspaper column. When he finally left the paper, after one row too many with the prince had taken its toll on his health, the column was well established and he and Anna were able to continue publishing it independently.

Demand for his novels continued. Both *Crime and Punishment* and *The Idiot* were reprinted, while Nekrasov, impressed by *The Devils*, made Dostoyevsky an offer for a new novel. By the time Dostoyevsky was ready to leave *The Citizen* he had been sufficiently reinvigorated to offer the publisher a new plot, and Nekrasov published *A Raw Youth* in *Notes of the Fatherland* in 1875.

Nekrasov's offer came as a surprise as, after *Poor Folk*, there had been little love lost between the two men. Nekrasov, however, was willing to recognize talent when he saw it and he was wise enough to go back on some of the things he had said when Dostoyevsky had disappointed him with his second novel, *The Double*. Nekrasov, always the astute businessman, offered Dostoyevsky more than Dostoyevsky's usual publisher, Katkov, could. Katkov had just bought *Anna Karenina* from Tolstoy and did not have enough cash to top Nekrasov's offer, probably feeling he could rely on Dostoyevsky because the author had already sent him the first half of the novel. Nekrasov was delighted with his triumph, although the novel is not counted among Dostoyevsky's greatest works. When he died in 1878 he was reconciled with Dostoyevsky and seemed convinced, as he was at the beginning of both their careers, that Dostoyevsky was a genius.

Dostoyevsky had not left *The Citizen* only to write *A Raw Youth*, nor because he saw it was possible to publish the *Diary of a Writer* on his own. He left because the pressures of editing a weekly newspaper were aggravating his already failing health. Now in his early fifties, he was living with the results of years of late nights, hard labour, violent fits and — perhaps most of all — constant chain-smoking of strong cigarettes. His general health was breaking down and he was developing the first signs of emphysema. Unable to carry on working in this way, with a hacking cough and breathing difficulties, Dostoyevsky left his post at *The Citizen*. He did not, however, forget to serve the brief prison sentence imposed for his publisher's oversight in quoting the Tsar. Anna had also suffered some difficulties during this time. Her sister had died of typhoid and her own life had been threatened by the development of a large boil on her neck.

The fact that Dostoyevsky left *The Citizen* did not automatically give the family more time together. In the summer of 1875 Dostoyevsky had to suffer separation from his family once again, this time going to the spa at Bad Ems in Germany where he could get medical treatment for his condition.

[1] *Dostoevsky: Portrayed by His Wife — The Diary and Reminiscences of Mme. Dostoevsky*, page 140.

[2] *Ibid*, page 139.

[3] Letter to Anna Dostoyevsky, July 1873, *Dostoyevsky: A Self Portrait*, page 204.

[4] Letter to A.G. Snitkina, June/July 1874, *Dostoyevsky: A Self Portrait*, page 206.

Chapter Eighteen
THE DREAM

Dostoyevsky's *Diary of a Writer* was published between 1873 and 1877, with a further special issue in 1881. It is not one of his better-known works in the popular market because much of it is opinion and contemporary comment. However, it contains several famous short stories, and it explains much of what is known about Dostoyevsky's early life. *Diary of a Writer* is the temperature gauge of the development of Dostoyevsky's religious thought at that time. In it he was working out the themes that he was to encapsulate in his last great novel, *The Brothers Karamazov*.

Diary of a Writer gave Dostoyevsky an opportunity to make money from his writing without putting pressure on him to write fiction, which required not only time but the strength of a good idea and a strong plot, for a living. At last he could give adequate time to his fiction and perhaps it is no coincidence that *The Brothers Karamazov*, conceived and written not long after the publication of the *Diary*, has been critically acclaimed throughout the world as the pinnacle of Dostoyevsky's achievement. The Dostoyevsky finances were by no means secure but the *Diary* provided sufficient leeway to give him some choice about what he did next.

The *Diary* was any writer's dream: a forum for the writer's opinion about anything that took his fancy. He was his own editor as well as the only contributor. The *Diary* was, as ever, limited by the censors, but Dostoyevsky was so loyal a citizen now that he rarely transgressed in the eyes of the authorities. In fact it was a good chance for him to expiate his early revolutionary sins. He was able to explain to his readers, one of whom was the Tsar, his present beliefs by exposing and criticizing his previous political and non-Christian philosophies.

In the *Diary* he recounts much of what is known about his relationship with Belinsky. He retells the story of that first night when he met the great critic — how for years he had admired Belinsky from afar and then found himself face to face with the great man's own admiration for him and his novel *Poor Folk*: "'But do you, yourself, understand," he repeated to me several times, screaming, as was his habit, "what you have written!" He always screamed when he spoke in a state of great agitation.'[1] Now many years removed from the sudden fame, followed just as quickly by the sudden split with this man, Dostoyevsky was able to reminisce with humour.

Dostoyevsky also used the *Diary* to criticize his own past, to denounce his former beliefs and to outline his own manifesto for the future. Even while reorganizing his political beliefs, however, he never lost his love or sympathy for the people of Russia, the peasants. When some critics suggested that peasants may also have had character defects, Dostoyevsky turned on them with the passion of one who has experienced more than any of them could know: 'So, don't tell me that I do not know the people! I know them: it was because of them that I again received into my soul Christ, Who had been revealed to me in my parents' home and Whom I was about to lose when, on my part, I transformed myself into a "European liberal"!'[2] Dostoyevsky credited the people with his salvation; their expression of the Christian faith had opened his eyes and they were crucial to his theories of Russian Christianity which he expanded later in the *Diary*.

He was, however, not blind to man's inhumanity to man, of whatever class. For years Dostoyevsky had taken an active interest in crime, not so much for fictional purposes, although his knowledge informed his novels, but because he had a keen sense of justice and was able to see that justice was not easy to dispense.

In the first few pages of the *Diary* he describes in harrowing detail the treatment of a young woman peasant by her husband: 'At length she grows quiet; she shrieks no longer; now she merely groans wildly; her breath comes in gasps every minute; but right then the blows come down more frequently, more violently . . .

Suddenly he throws away the strap; like a madman, he seizes a stick, a bough, anything, and breaks it over her back with three last, terrific, blows. — No more! He quits, plants himself by the table, sighs, and sets himself to his Kvass.'[3]

The young woman finally gathered the courage to go to the police and report her husband's treatment of her. They replied that they could do nothing and suggested that she should learn to live 'amicably' with her husband. Driven to despair she committed suicide, but her suicide solved nothing. Since the husband had not been charged or convicted, the little daughter who watched the maltreatment of her mother would soon become the next victim of his violence. Thus the violence would be perpetuated down the generations.

Though Dostoyevsky was moved to pity for the woman, he was not unaware of what might be today called 'contributory factors'. He knew only too well what conditions such peasants had to endure. Small one-roomed cottages, mudwalled or perhaps wood, were their only accommodation and their lives were a constant struggle against starvation and ill-treatment. Since their so-called liberation the serfs' situation had grown substantially worse, not better. Small wonder then that men were driven to violence. But, Dostoyevsky points out, if the conditions cause the violence, why isn't every peasant beating his wife?

As a young man he had hoped that a perfect environment would create a perfect man. In prison he learned that human nature is much more complex than he had suspected. On one hand, among his fellow prisoners were murderers 'who were so gay and so carefree that one might have made a bet that their consciences never for a moment reproached them.'[4] On the other hand, men whom he had come to regard as wild beasts 'would manifest such a wealth of fine feeling, so keen a comprehension of the sufferings of others, seen in the light of the consciousness of their own, that one could almost fancy that scales had fallen from one's eyes.'[5]

This apparently contradictory view of the common people is evident in his comments in the *Diary*. Millions of peasants, he points out, live perfectly decent and honest lives, despite the fact that they are ground down by the ever-present threat of starvation. Others, however, succumb to temptation. Why? How much does environment contribute to crime? How much are the individuals themselves to blame for their crimes, and how much is society to blame? It was these questions that Dostoyevsky debated openly in the *Diary*. Through the *Diary* he even became actively involved in a case by virtue of the opinion he expressed.

A young woman, Yekaterina Kornilova, threw her six-year-old stepdaughter out a fourth-floor window. Kornilova, pregnant at the time, had just had a row with her husband and wanted to get at him, so she flung his little girl out the window and then went straight to the police to confess. Extraordinarily enough, the child survived with only a mild concussion, but since Kornilova had confessed to the child's murder the police charged her with attempted murder. She was convicted of that crime, although the first conviction was rescinded on a technicality, and Dostoyevsky became interested in the retrial.

Dostoyevsky protested against the initial conviction. In his article he argued that her pregnancy may have affected her mind. Pregnancy paranoia, post-natal depression, and their cousin in hormonal disturbances, pre-menstrual tension, are phenomena well-known to the medical profession now. However, even today some experts will deny the relevance of these conditions to women's actions. But Dostoyevsky felt that her pregnant state was an important factor, and in many ways he was ahead of his time. His article caused a great deal of public controversy. At the retrial expert evidence was called in and Kornilova was acquitted, despite the fact that the judge warned the jury not to be too influenced by the open debate that Dostoyevsky had provoked.

Dostoyevsky's understanding of the criminal mind, evident in *Crime and Punishment* and in *The Devils*, had won him great respect. He was always concerned to understand the motivation and circumstances behind evil acts. He was always seeking for the just solution, although he was the first to agree that justice did not always mean acquittal. An unpunished crime was unfair to both the perpetrator and victim. He protested this in an article he wrote when a woman who slashed her husband's lover was acquitted on the grounds that it was a crime of passion. The defence lawyer pleaded that she would have been less than a woman if she had not slashed her unfaithful husband's lover, and the judge agreed with him. Dostoyevsky said that by letting her off they were condoning the crime and therefore encouraging the woman to be less than human, for part of being human was the ability to control oneself and to take responsibility for one's actions. Criminals must be made responsible for their crimes.

Although much of the *Diary* was comment on contemporary events, occasionally Dostoyevsky included a short imaginative piece, such as, the story of the man who lies down on a gravestone just after a funeral and listens to the voices of the dead talking in their graves beneath him. In his waking dream the listener hears the newly dead talk to one another until, after a few months in their limbo world, they fall silent again. The story faces Dostoyevsky's own fear of being buried alive; in his youth he had feared this so much that he left instructions that, in case of his death, everyone must wait a week before burying him, in order to be sure that he was dead.

To regular readers of the *Diary* the short stories must have come as a pleasant relief after much intense comment on current affairs. At least two of the stories, 'The Dream of a Ridiculous Man' and 'At Christ's Christmas Tree', indicate the state of Dostoyevsky's faith. The latter, a Russian equivalent to 'The Little Match Girl' by Hans Christian Andersen, tells the story of a little boy who runs out in the city streets after his mother dies. It is Christmas and outside it is bitterly cold and snowing. The little boy has never been in the city before and he is delighted by the window displays, the mechanical puppets and the tantalizing smells of food. At last, tired and cold, he settles down behind a pile of wood in a yard and goes to sleep. All at once his mother comes to get him and takes him to Christ's Christmas tree because, so the other children who are gathered at the tree tell the little boy, Jesus always has a Christmas party for little boys and girls who have no tree of their own. In the morning, of course, a cold stiff little body is found amid a pile of wood. The story moistened the eye of every Russian who read it and although it is not as well known as many similar stories it is indeed a children's classic.

'The Dream of a Ridiculous Man' has a far more sinister atmosphere. The ridiculous man, who is contemplating suicide, dreams that he commits the act and that in death he flies far beyond the earth to another planet. On that planet he finds that the inhabitants have not yet sinned. Inevitably they do not survive the visit of their sinful friend unscathed, although for centuries the dreamer lives among them in peace. But, says the dreamer, 'In the end I corrupted the lot of them! How I managed to do it, I can't say; I don't remember too clearly. My dream flashed through eons, leaving in me only a general impression of the whole. All I know is that I caused their fall from grace. Like a sinister trichina, like a plague germ contaminating whole kingdoms . . . They learned how to lie, they came to love it, and they grew to appreciate the beauty of untruth.'[6]

In the end they cannot remember a time when they did not sin, and they do not believe the dreamer when he assures them that it is so. When the dreamer awakes he is a changed man, rather like Scrooge in Dickens' *A Christmas Carol*. He concludes that there is only one way to live — to love others as you love yourself. 'And that's all there is to it. Nothing else is required. That would settle everything . . . And I shall fight it. And if everyone wanted it, everything could be arranged immediately.'[7] The dreamer has become a preacher of a fundamentally Christian message.

Dostoyevsky's return to faith was marked by some exploration of the less orthodox aspects of Russian Christianity. Much religious practice in Russia was superstitious. Christianity was a blend of the old folk religion with its ancient legends and the modern stories of the coming of Christ and the activity of the saints. As most of the population lived on a knife edge, many turned to superstition and folk religion to help solve their problems. Dostoyevsky also found comfort in some of these solutions, at least at first. After Maria Isayeva left Semipalatinsk with her husband, he had consulted a fortune teller, and this stirred an interest in spiritualism that fascinated him for some years.

During his four-year stay abroad with Anna, he read the works of Swedenborg who, after a spiritual experience, claimed he had witnessed societies of spiritual beings functioning in civilizations much like those on earth. When Dostoyevsky returned from Europe he began to investigate more thoroughly the possibility of contact with the dead. He attended seances, at the time the fashionable thing to do. St Petersburg was well populated with mediums; there were so many seances that a government inquiry was set up to investigate them. The inquiry concluded that the seances were a fraud. Dostoyevsky was not entirely convinced, for he had even held a seance with his wife and children which he claimed worked without the help of deception. However, he could not ignore the Bible's explicit condemnation of spiritualism. His desire to contact another dimension, however possible, was condemned by the Christian faith he now believed in.

In the *Diary* he at last renounced spiritualism, using the government's report as the occasion for his own comments. 'Briefly, spiritism is undoubtedly a great, extraordinary and most foolish fallacy, a lecherous doctrine and ignorance; but the trouble is that all this, perhaps does not transpire around the table as the Committee order us to believe, and, indeed, it is also impossible to call all spiritists humbugs and fools . . . The mystical meaning of spiritism — this most harmful thing — should have been taken into particular consideration. Yet the Committee has not given thought to this particular significance. Of course, under no circumstance, would it have been in a position to crush the evil; but at least, by different — not so naive and haughty — methods the Committee could have inculcated in spiritists even a respect for its findings, while it could have exercised a strong influence on the wavering followers of spiritism.'[8]

In his last novel, *The Brothers Karamazov*, Dostoyevsky has a humorous dig at the spiritists: when the devil appears to Ivan, he remarks how fond he is of spiritists. The presence of an immortal soul in each human being has a more serious side: immortality implies responsibility. In *The Brothers Karamazov* and in the *Diary* Dostoyevsky is not afraid to suggest that some things are immoral and dangerous because of their possible effect on the immortal soul.

In April 1876 the Bulgarians rebelled against the Turkish Empire but the Ottomans crushed the uprising quickly and with cruelty. The atrocities they committed on Bulgarian civilians enraged Russia and shocked Europe. For a short time, Turkey had no allies in Western Europe and so was vulnerable to Russian action. In Serbia a similar uprising took place and in Moscow prayers were said on behalf of the Serbs. However, despite some help from Russian volunteers, this uprising was also put down.

The Pan-Slavic movement in Russia, which received the support of the Orthodox church, felt it was a Christian's duty to show solidarity with their persecuted brothers under Turkish rule. In England and other Western European countries fears grew that, should the Turkish Empire collapse, Russia would sweep in and invade so much of the fallen Empire that it would become too powerful in Europe. Initially Russia tried to get promises from the Ottomans that the rights of Christians would be respected and they could consider themselves under the authority of the Metropolitan of Moscow in religious matters. European diplomats attempted to get both countries to agree to a treaty, but the Turks wanted no interference, and on 24 April 1877 Russia declared war on Turkey. By January 1878 the Russians looked set to invade Constantinople. However, an armistice was agreed which prevented this and a treaty was signed that set up an independent state of Bulgaria and ceded the Caucasus to Russia. This agreement did not go far enough for many Pan-Slavists, including Dostoyevsky. Dostoyevsky believed that Russia's political ambitions were inextricably linked with its Christian mission.

When its emperor converted to Christianity in AD 321 Constantinople had been the capital of the Roman Empire. As a result of the Emperor Constantine's conversion it became the capital of the Christian empire, Christendom. The form of Christian faith that emanated from that source was therefore purer and more orthodox than the later forms of Christianity that developed in Rome and throughout the Reformation. It was this tradition that the Russian Orthodox church followed. Therefore the invasion by Russia of Constantinople would restore to Christianity the original capital of Christendom and Russia would be the state that ruled it.

As early as June 1876 Dostoyevsky was so excited by the success of the military campaign against the Turks that he predicted that Russia would take Constantinople, thus restoring to Christendom its original capital. A new faith would evolve which would be Christianity in its purest form: 'this would be a genuine exaltation of Christ's truth preserved in the East, a new exaltation of Christ's cross and the final word of Orthodoxy, which is headed by Russia.'[9]

Nine months later, Dostoyevsky had to concede that Russia would not soon take Constantinople but this did not distract him from what had come to be his creed: it was Russia's mission to restore proper faith in the world. Both Roman Catholicism and Protestantism had failed to proclaim the true message of Christianity. 'Catholicism sold Christ when it blessed the Jesuits and sanctioned the righteousness "of every means for Christ's cause"' he wrote.[10] Catholicism had chosen to perpetuate Christianity by earthly means. It used the methods of the Spanish Inquisition to convert people to its creed. The Pope considered himself an earthly ruler and wanted political, not spiritual, power.

Dostoyevsky particularly abhorred the doctrine of papal infallibility propounded in 1870. He wrote a satirical speech for the Pope that expressed what Dostoyevsky believed the Pope really wanted: 'So you thought that I was satisfied with the mere title of King of the Papal State? Know that I have ever considered myself potentate of the whole world and over all earthly kings . . . and sovereign over all sovereigns, and to me alone on earth belong the destinies, the ages and the bounds of time. And now I am proclaiming this in the dogma of my infallibility.'[11]

Dostoyevsky feared an aggressive Catholicism. He believed socialism was an inevitable consequence of living in proximity to Catholicism. The Catholic church at that time offered little earthly reward to its people. Millions suffered great injustice while the Catholic church did nothing to alleviate their earthly suffering, on the grounds that they would be compensated in the life hereafter. The consequences of the evil of Catholicism were clear enough in France: first the revolution and then the Paris Commune.

Dostoyevsky was little more impressed with Protestantism than with Catholicism. At least the Protestants had some educational value. But industrialization, science and secularization were the inevitable consequences of Protestant thought and they too led to atheism. The inevitable consequence of Protestantism, that is the work ethic combined with a negative rationale, resulted in modes of thinking that were guided by scientific method and this that led to secularization. This was a process that Dostoyevsky felt he could already see taking place in Western Europe, particularly in Germany and England.

Dostoyevsky predicted that the two great representative nations of Catholicism and Protestantism, France and Germany, would go to war. Germany would defeat France and, once dominant, would collapse. Then Russia could convert and dominate both weakened nations. In view of events in the twentieth century it could be argued that he was not far wrong, although the creed the Russians carried with them owed more to Belinsky than to Orthodoxy.

Meanwhile Dostoyevsky wrote in favour of the Bulgarians and against the Turks. The treatment of the Bulgarians by the Turks was barbaric, and Dostoyevsky retold the stories of torture in graphic detail. Women were raped and pregnant women disembowelled; babies were bounced on Turkish bayonets while their doomed mothers watched. It was a matter of honour that Russia, an Eastern Orthodox state, saw to it that these people were protected and rescued.

Dostoyevsky asserted that the war against Islam proved that the Russian people possessed the purest form of Christianity there was. He cited the example of the peasant Foma Danilov, martyred by the Turks because he would not renounce Christ. Danilov's act was entirely unselfish: he could not have known that his cruel martyrdom would become public knowledge, that his death would make him a hero. If he had renounced Christ and saved his life, who would have known? Here was a true Russian Christian able to sacrifice himself to a cruel fate for the sake of Christ and the honour of his country. The Russian people and the Slavs were inextricably linked both religiously and racially and the Russians were therefore obliged to defend their brothers. Defence of the Slavs was the only honourable course for an Orthodox Christian nation.

'Undeniably, there lives in the people the firm belief that Russia exists for the sole purpose of serving Christ and protecting ecumenic Orthodoxy *as a whole*', wrote Dostoyevsky.[12] If Russia lost its integrity in this matter, it would be severely weakened if not destroyed. 'To abandon the Slavic idea and to leave without solution the problem entailing the fate of Eastern Christianity (N.B. which is the substance of the Eastern problem) — would be equivalent to smashing Russia into pieces, and to inventing in her place something new, but not Russia at all.'[13]

As he continued to write his column, Dostoyevsky had to revise some of his opinions. Russia did not invade Turkey or take Constantinople. Neither France nor Germany looked substantially weakened or likely to go to war with each other again. The Catholic community's loyalty to the Pope was as strong as ever.

The settlement of the 'Eastern Question' was not to be as simple as Dostoyevsky had envisaged, but he had now established a creed from which he would not depart. The Russian community of peasant Christians, linked to God through their affinity with the simple life of the soil, could redeem Christianity for Russia and thence for the world. Dostoyevsky wanted the Christianity he had come to acknowledge to contribute to a better society, rather than to point only to a distant Kingdom of Heaven, achieved by not complaining on earth. He may have criticized the Pope for coveting earthly power, but he saw no contradiction in urging Russia to take that very power to facilitate the spread of Orthodoxy. This, in fact, was Russia's mission: 'Let at the same time our faith grow still firmer that precisely herein lies Russia's genuine mission, her strength and truth, and that the self-sacrifice for the oppressed and forsaken by everybody in Europe, in the interests of civilization, is a real service to its actual and true interests.

'Nay, it is necessary that in political organisms the same Christ's truth must be preserved; some nation at least must radiate. Otherwise what would happen? Everything would be dimmed, distorted and would be drowned in cynicism. Otherwise you would be unable to restrain the morality of individual citizens, too, and in this event how is the entire organism of the people going to live? Authority is needed. It is necessary that the sun shine. The sun appeared in the East, and it is from the East that the new day begins for mankind.'[14]

[1] 'Russian Satire'; 'Virgin Soil'; 'Last Songs'; 'Old Reminiscences', *Diary of a Writer*, page 587.

[2] 'Concerning One Most Important Matter', *Diary of a Writer*, page 984.

THE DREAM

[3] 'The Milieu', *Diary of a Writer*, page 19.

[4] *House of the Dead*, page 10.

[5] *Ibid*, page 258.

[6] *Notes from the Underground, White Nights, The Dream of a Ridiculous Man and Selections from The House of the Dead*, page 220.

[7] *Ibid*, pages 225–26.

[8] 'Again But One Word About Spiritism', *Diary of a Writer*, page 306.

[9] 'The Utopian Conception of History', *Diary of a Writer*, page 365.

[10] 'It is Necessary to Seize the Moment', *Diary of a Writer*, page 911.

[11] 'Dead Force and Future Forces', *Diary of a Writer*, page 256.

[12] 'Where Does the Business Stand?', *Diary of a Writer*, page 555.

[13] 'Mollusks Taken for Human Beings . . . ', *Diary of a Writer*, page 842.

[14] 'The Metternichs and the Don Quixotes', *Diary of a Writer*, page 609.

Chapter Nineteen

THE BROTHERS

'My dear Katerina Fyodorovna, do you believe in Christ and His promises? If you do (or wish to believe very much), give yourself up to him fully and the torments of this dichotomy will be greatly alleviated and you will obtain spiritual consolation.'[1]

This was an answer to one of the steady stream of letters Dostoyevsky was now receiving in response to the *Diary of a Writer*. His correspondent complained of suffering from the duality that Dostoyevsky so ably portrayed in his characterizations. She was painfully aware of the division between the 'is' and the 'ought' in her own life. Dostoyevsky pointed her to Christ and also recommended art and creativity as a good cure for painful memories. As a result of his advice Katerina Fyodorovna went on to write an autobiography that made her famous.

Dostoyevsky carried on a conscientious correspondence with his readers, answering as many letters as he could. To one woman, at a loss as to how to educate her daughter in good literature and ideas; he sent a reading list including his old favourites — Dickens, Walter Scott and Pushkin. He also recommended Turgenev, although not until the daughter was a little bit older. To another mother he suggested that she teach the gospel to her son through her own example and goodness.

Not all the letters Dostoyevsky received were complimentary. One woman accused him of squandering his talent on the *Diary* instead of focusing it on his novels. Dostoyevsky replied that he was always observing life and that he was using the *Diary* to recount it and order it. A more serious charge was levelled by a correspondent who took him to task for his anti-Semitic statements, which were particularly vitriolic in the *Diary*: 'I should like to know why are you protesting against the Yiddisher, and not the exploiter in general? . . . Is it possible that *you* are unable to lift yourself to the comprehension of the fundamental law of any social life to the effect that *all* citizens of a state, without any exception, if they are paying all taxes required for the existence of the state must enjoy *all* rights and advantages of its existence?[2]

Dostoyevsky believed in Jewish conspiracy theories that were prevalent in his day and, sadly, he uncritically accepted every evil story about the Jews that ever came to his attention. In America, he said, they corrupted the liberated slaves, and in Lithuania they blackmailed the locals. He assured the Jewish community that he did not hate them on religious grounds: his prejudice, he said, did not stem from the fact that Judas sold Christ. He insisted that it was the Jews' behaviour that made him despise them, and he cited these stories as the proof. 'Ask the native population in our border regions: What is propelling the Jew — has been propelling him for centuries? You will receive a unanimous answer: *mercilessness*.'[3]

His attitude was by no means a minority view or a socially unacceptable one. It was common all over Europe to believe that the Jews were a threat to social stability, that they were cruel, godless and money grabbing. Anti-Semitism, built on centuries of prejudice, was almost a mark of respectability; no Christian would dream of suggesting any other theory. The Jewish man who wrote to Dostoyevsky admired his work and believed that his genius could extend to examining the Jewish question with the perspicacity that he applied to the more general human condition. It seemed surprising to the writer that Dostoyevsky could portray a murderer's psychology so accurately and yet cling to his damaging prejudices about the Jews.

He hoped that Dostoyevsky might be able to break out of his conditioning and reveal anti-Jewish prejudice as a fraud. But for all Dostoyevsky's understanding of human psychological motivations, in this instance he was blinded by his love of Russia and his devotion to the Orthodox church, and he accepted the reactionary opinion that the Jews were enemies of these institutions.

In spite of the anti-Semitism in the *Diary*, Dostoyevsky did not make Jews the villains in his novels. The novels are famous for exposing bigotry, small-mindedness and fanaticism. For example, in *The Devils* one of the conspirators, the Jew Lyamshin, is no more evil that the rest of them. When the gang comes to commit the murder it is Lyamshin who loses control and is unable to do it. It would be true to say that none of Dostoyevsky's prejudice is present in his novels, but in the novels polemic is not his main concern. Although some characters do express anti-Semitic views, Dostoyevsky's fundamental concern is human psychology and the existence of God.

Now in his late fifties, Dostoyevsky prefaced every letter he wrote with an apology for the delay, explaining that he was hampered by ill-health. In 1877 he had set himself a programme of projects to be completed before his death: to write a book about Jesus Christ, a Russian *Candide*, a classic poem and his memoirs. By 1880 Dostoyevsky had realized none of these ambitions but he was writing his last great novel, *The Brothers Karamazov*, where he most scrupulously represented the mechanisms of human psychology and belief.

Sigmund Freud wrote that *The Brothers Karamazov* was the most 'magnificent novel ever written'[4], a book that could hardly be over-praised. His admiration, though, was generally limited to Dostoyevsky's immensely complex but authentic psychological studies of the characters. Here was an author who understood human psychological motivations and explored them in depth. What Dostoyevsky had to say about God Freud dismissed as a part of the author's neuroticism. Nevertheless, Dostoyevsky wanted to say a great deal about God and the nature of faith in this novel.

The novel, an almost 1,000-page long family saga, is set in a small rural community in Russia. It centres on the fortunes of three brothers, sons of the debauched and lecherous Fyodor Karamazov. The Karamazov brothers all have a zest for life but they are tainted by the family wickedness, exemplified in its worst excesses by the father. Dmitry, the oldest son, is most like his father: sensual, impetuous, lustful and too quick to spend his inheritance. Ivan and Alyosha are Dmitry's half-brothers, the sons of a different mother. Ivan is an agnostic sunk in despair and angry with a God he does not believe in. Alyosha is his antithesis: joyful, healthy and religious but also a realist. He has spent some years in a local monastery as a novice and, as the story begins, he is about to go back out into the world.

As literary figures, each brother has a prototype in Dostoyevsky's earlier work or experience. Alyosha is a more successful version of the 'idiot', Prince Myshkin. He brings positive Christian values into the story but, unlike the prince, he is not afraid of action, nor is his presence divisive. At the end of the story he brings about reconciliation between Dmitry and Katerina, with whom Dmitry's relationship was stormy. Ivan is a more realistic version of that earliest of Dostoyevsky's anti-heroes, the 'double' Golyadkin. Ivan is divided in his mind. He does not believe in God and yet he fights against him. He believes that any action is permitted, because without God there are no moral constraints, and yet he acts as if there are such constraints. He does not believe in the supernatural and yet he sees the devil in his room — or is the devil really the other side of himself? Like the 'double', Ivan is brought face to face with his other side.

Dmitry's prototype is slightly different: it is taken from real life. Dostoyevsky's daughter believed that the evil Fyodor Karamazov was modelled on her grandfather. Just who the old man was modelled on may not be certain, but what is known is that Dostoyevsky's use of parricide in the novel had far more to do with a convict he met while serving his sentence in Siberia. Prince Ilyinsky, Dostoyevsky's fellow prisoner in Siberia, had been falsely convicted of murdering his father. Dostoyevsky was fascinated by the miscarriage of justice, and he bestowed a similar fate on Dmitry Karamazov. The plot surrounding Dmitry is simple. He has the motive for killing his father and all the evidence points to him as the murderer. In the end he goes to Siberia for the crime. In fact, however, it was committed by Smerdyakov, believed to be the illegitimate son of Fyodor Karamazov and a retarded woman whom he raped. Smerdyakov, an epileptic, murdered the old man and used an epileptic fit as an alibi.

Ivan Karamazov is a different matter. He wants his father dead. He believes that in a godless world everything is permitted. Smerdyakov puts two and two together and murders old Karamazov himself. He gives enough warning to persuade him to leave town on the day he has chosen for the murder. Ivan is not fully cognisant of what is going on; once he realizes what has happened he takes the guilt upon himself. Like Stavrogin in *The Devils*, whose wife and family were murdered by default, Ivan believes that he has somehow instigated his father's murder by not acting to prevent it. Moreover, in contrast to his earlier belief, he now realizes that not everything can be permitted and he goes mad trying to exonerate his brother. Smerdyakov hangs himself without confessing to the authorities, thereby denying the brothers their only chance to prove Dmitry's innocence.

Despite the dismal fates of these characters *The Brothers Karamazov* is one of Dostoyevsky's more optimistic novels. This is because of the presence of Alyosha and his teacher, Father Zossima, an 'elder' at a nearby monastery. As the antithesis to Ivan, Alyosha believes in God and therefore believes in an absolute morality — not everything can be permitted because God would not permit it and people must act according to God's judgment. Just as Ivan is presented with a challenge to his creed by the appearance of the devil in his room, Alyosha's beliefs are also tested.

When his spiritual mentor, Father Zossima, dies his body begins to smell of decay within twenty-four hours of his death. This is not the miracle that people of simple faith looked for to affirm that the revered monk was indeed a saint. Confirmation of sainthood would be looked for in quite the opposite sign, lack of decay for instance, or a healing miracle at the coffin. Alyosha has to come to terms with the fact that even though God exists he has permitted something that those who follow him would not. As he kneels beside the stinking coffin he prays for enlightenment and finds himself transported to the scene of the wedding at Cana. At the feast he sees Father Zossima. The old man rebukes him gently for being surprised that he is there. The smell from the coffin is not a sign of God's displeasure: Father Zossima is a part of God's kingdom. As he did in life, Father Zossima repeats his instruction to Alyosha to leave the monastery and take the new wine to the people in the world outside. Just as the wedding at Cana was a miracle in a secular world, so Alyosha's vocation is in the secular environment rather than within the confines of the monastery. It is Alyosha who counters many of the doubts expressed by Ivan, whose literary function is to challenge belief in the existence of God.

In the *Diary of a Writer* Dostoyevsky was explicit about his religious beliefs; he is less so in the novels. He was not unaware of the detrimental effect didacticism could have on a story but, in his account of Father Zossima's life and the repetition of some of his sermons, much of Dostoyevsky's theology may be discerned.

In 'The Dream of the Ridiculous Man' Dostoyevsky had brought his hero back to earth with the realization that if only everyone loved one another then the earth could be paradise. Father Zossima also proclaims the necessity of love: 'Brothers, be not afraid of men's sins. Love man even in his sin, for that already bears the semblance of divine love and is the highest love on earth. Love all God's creation, the whole of it and every grain of sand. Love every leaf, every ray of God's light! Love the animals, love the plants, love everything. If you love everything you will perceive the divine mystery in things.'[5]

Not only should love motivate man; so should responsibility. Men are responsible for each other. Cain should have been his brother's keeper. 'Remember particularly that you cannot be a judge of anyone. For there can be no judge of a felon on earth, until the judge himself recognizes that he is just such a felon as the man standing before him, and that perhaps he is more than anyone responsible for the crime of the man in the dock.'[6] Brotherhood, mutual responsibility and love are the recipe for an earthly and Christian utopia. In the *Diary of a Writer* Dostoyevsky pictured these qualities emanating from the unique faith of the Russian people. In his sermons Father Zossima echoes this. Nevertheless, Russian nationalist theology is not a major theme in *The Brothers Karamazov*.

The fundamental issue in the novel is the place of suffering and sin in God's world. Through Father Zossima, Dostoyevsky attempts to answer the questions raised by the co-existence of God's love and human misery. Love makes the world into an earthly paradise by making people good to one another. Even so, paradoxically, suffering and sin also have a necessary place in this world. Father Zossima reads Jesus' words in John 12:24: 'Verily, verily, I say unto you, Except a corn of wheat fall into the ground and die, it abideth alone; but if it die, it bringeth forth much fruit.' This verse, later placed on Dostoyevsky's tombstone, is the key to his religious thinking. Dostoyevsky suggests that sin is necessary because without suffering there can be no individuality or true happiness. Happiness without knowledge is nothing more than ignorance. Dostoyevsky is aware of the difficulties that this theory presents and he voices his own doubts through Ivan.

In a discussion with Alyosha, Ivan cites the suffering of children as the greatest stumbling block to faith. It is not so much that Ivan does not believe in God as that he disagrees with his priorities: 'Listen: if all have to suffer so as to buy eternal harmony by their suffering, what have the children to do with it — tell me, please? It is entirely incomprehensible why they, too, should have to suffer and why they should have to buy harmony by their sufferings.'[7] Listening to Ivan, even Alyosha concedes that he cannot tolerate the suffering of children. In fact, Ivan's arguments are so cogent that they almost eclipse the novel's aim — to affirm, not challenge, the existence of God and the truth of Christianity.

Dostoyevsky realized this; he wrote that in attempting to present the pro and contra arguments relating to Christianity he had been rather more successful with the contra than with the pro, which was not his intention. Dostoyevsky reassured a friend in a letter written in May 1879: 'My hero's blasphemy will be triumphantly refuted in the next (June) number for which I am now working in fear and trembling and with reverence, since I think the task (the defeat of anarchism) I have set myself would be a feat of heroism.'[8]

Alyosha counters Ivan's claims by pointing to Christ. Because Christ was innocent and suffered terribly he has bought the right to forgive man his terrible sins. God's justice is forgiveness and this somehow compensates for or even justifies the suffering. Here Dostoyevsky introduces the chapter that has become one of contemporary literature's most famous fables, 'The Grand Inquisitor'. Ivan Karamazov, the fictional author of the piece, calls it his poem. It sits just a little uncomfortably in the text because it addresses an issue not entirely relevant to the discussion on suffering. It is more relevant to Dostoyevsky's own debates about Christ, many years before, in the Belinsky circle.

In 'The Grand Inquisitor' Christ himself returns to sixteenth-century Seville when the atrocities of the Spanish Inquisition are at their peak. It is a time when people are converted to Christianity under the threat of unspeakable torture and a fiery death. Needless to say, the incarnate Christ with his humble preaching is not popular with the authorities and the Grand Inquisitor throws him in gaol, only to visit him at night to discuss the differences between them. The Grand Inquisitor accuses Christ of not succumbing to the wilderness temptations: he did not turn the stones into bread, take earthly power or perform miracles in order to win people's faith. The Roman Catholic church, on the other hand, says the Grand Inquisitor, has done all those things and so has been a good deal more effective in subjugating people and winning their loyalty. 'You promised them bread from heaven, but, I repeat again, can it compare with earthly bread in the eyes of the weak, always vicious and always ignoble race of man?'9

The Grand Inquisitor assures Christ that man is a good deal happier being ruled and so deprived of free will and responsibility: 'Instead of gaining possession of men's freedom, you gave them greater freedom than ever! Or did you forget that a tranquil mind and even death is dearer to man than the free choice in the knowledge of good and evil?'10 Man, says this sinister figure, is fundamentally a weak creature and the church looks after the weak by telling them what to do. It is, of course, the Roman Catholic church that Dostoyevsky accuses of this crime. In reply to Ivan, all Alyosha can do is defend Orthodoxy and deny its part in such crimes as the Inquisition.

In the fable of the Grand Inquisitor, the church no longer needs Christ or God, for it has the earthly power it needs to rule. The returned Christ is interfering with fifteen centuries of church domination and, inevitably, he must be burned. He is effaced by human evil just as Belinsky had said he would be when he and Dostoyevsky speculated as to how a contemporary Christ would function in modern Russia. Still, the image of Christ in 'The Grand Inquisitor' is not without power and Alyosha suggests that Ivan has written a poem in praise of Christ, not a disparagement of him.

The story of the Grand Inquisitor implies that in order to attain true happiness one must exercise free will and perhaps even sin in order to appreciate God's offered forgiveness and salvation. It also shows that most people do not want this free will and the responsibility it brings and so do not want the ultimate happiness they subsequently might achieve. That is not to say that Dostoyevsky advocated committing sin as a prelude to salvation but, ever since his time in Siberia, he accepted sin's inevitability in human nature.

It is in the forgiving spirit of children that Dostoyevsky finds hope at the end of *The Brothers Karamazov*. At the funeral of a small child, Ilyusha, whose bitter response to poverty and injustice made him an outcast among his friends and who died of consumption, the reconciliation of these friends takes place. The children have come to recognize the importance of forgiveness, of mutual responsibility and of love for one another, and they have found faith. "'Karamazov,'" cried Kolya, "is it really true that, as our religion tells us, we shall all rise from the dead and come to life and see one another again, all, and Ilyusha?"

"Certainly we shall rise again, certainly we shall see one another, and shall tell one another gladly and joyfully all that has been.'"[11]

[1] Letter to Yekaterina Yunge, April 1880, *Dostoyevsky's Occasional Writings*, page 309.

[2] 'The Jewish Question', *Diary of a Writer*, page 638.

[3] 'Status in Statu. Forty Centuries of Existence', *Diary of a Writer*, page 648.

[4] *Stavrogin's Confession*, page 87.

[5] *The Brothers Karamazov*, page 375.

[6] *Ibid*, page 378.

[7] *Ibid*, page 286.

[8] Letter to N.A. Lyabimov, May 1879, *Dostoyevsky: A Self Portrait*, page 220.

[9] *The Brothers Karamazov*, page 297.

[10] *Ibid*, page 298.

[11] *Ibid*, page 912.

Chapter Twenty
THE PROPHET

'You judge very rightly when you opine that I hold all evil to be grounded upon disbelief, and maintain that he who abjures nationalism, abjures faith also. That applies especially to Russia, for with us national consciousness is based on Christianity. "A Christian peasant people", "believing Russia": these are our fundamental conceptions. A Russian who abjures nationalism (and there are many such) is either an atheist or indifferent to religious questions.'[1]

In this letter to a Dr A.F. Blagonravov, Dostoyevsky encapsulates what he believed to be the relationship between Russia and Christianity. In one paragraph he discounts the faith of all but the most patriotic Russians and credits only Russia with a pure faith. Now, almost at the end of his life, Dostoyevsky was to have a chance to express this view to a larger public and, in one moment of glory, he was to offer the culmination of all his thinking to mother Russia.

By the end of the 1870s Dostoyevsky was famous enough to merit six lines in the Russian version of *Who's Who*; Turgenev, however, received twenty-four lines. Dostoyevsky was included in the honorary committee of the Association Littéraire where, once again, Turgenev was included but so also was Victor Hugo, one of Dostoyevsky's own favourites.

The sales of his books were increasing. *The Brothers Karamazov* was such a great success that Anna began to build up a mail-order company. Even so, money was still a problem for the Dostoyevskys. Fyodor never did get over his propensity to give money away to what he thought were deserving causes. This frustrated Anna and they argued frequently. Fyodor accused Anna of not looking after him properly. She accused him of being too free with their money, spending it on clothes and other people instead of his family and his debts.

Anna was not above using deceit to make sure her husband's affection was secure. She once wrote him an anonymous letter suggesting that she was having an affair with somebody else. In the letter she said that he should look in the locket that she wore around her neck and there he would see the likeness of her lover. Dostoyevsky's reaction was almost too gratifying. Obviously agitated, he stormed into her room and broke the necklace from around her neck. In the locket he found only a picture of himself. Anna explained her prank and Dostoyevsky was enraged. He warned her that he might have done something much more irresponsible than simply snatch away the locket.

Towards the end of his life, the couple spent much more time apart. Anna spent much time in Staraya Russa, which provided a better environment for the children, while Fyodor was often in Ems, from where he wrote anxious letters enquiring about the children's health. They were finally able to buy the small house in Staraya Russa and Dostoyevsky would join his family there when the demands of work did not keep him in St Petersburg or Moscow. In Staraya Russa he had time to write, to be with his children and to enjoy the life of a country gentleman. The local priest often visited and the family became a part of the community.

Among the Russian literary community it was well known that Dostoyevsky greatly admired the poet Pushkin. He had voiced his admiration for Pushkin at the grave of his old editor and rival, Nekrasov, and had then compared the talents of the two poets. His opinion had not been greeted with unanimous approval but his admiration for Pushkin never wavered. He often did public readings of Pushkin's work and his recitations were said to be hypnotic. He was the obvious choice, therefore, to unveil a memorial to Pushkin in Moscow in the spring of 1880. The occasion, a celebration of the writer's work, was also to be a gathering of Russia's literary giants. It was Dostoyevsky's chance to offer his views to a wider public; it was also a major honour.

He accepted the invitation to unveil the memorial and to

address an audience at a dinner to be held during that week. His correspondence with his wife suggests that she might have liked to go with him, but Dostoyevsky preferred to be on his own.

Dostoyevsky arrived in Moscow on the 24th of May ready for the ceremony which was to follow several days later. The other writers were now gathered in Moscow waiting to hear if the ceremony would continue, as the death of the Tsarina had delayed it. Instead of the celebration of the 26th the writers decided to occupy the time by giving a dinner in Dostoyevsky's honour. There were six speeches, Dostoyevsky wrote to Anna, some of them very long. At last his contribution to literature was being recognized.

Dostoyevsky was not the only author taking part in the Pushkin celebration. Turgenev had also been allocated a slot in the programme of events. Even after nearly forty years none of their old enmity had abated. Dostoyevsky was hurt by being excluded from a dinner arranged in Turgenev's honour. Worse, he was not present at the meeting which finalized all the arrangements for the meetings in Pushkin's honour. Dostoyevsky was allocated Pushkin's poem 'The Prophet' to read when he would have preferred another.

The night of 8 June was to be Dostoyevsky's triumph. That night he gave a speech, published in a special edition of the *Diary of a Writer*, lauding Pushkin as the greatest Russian poet because he affirmed the great Russian virtues of Christianity, affinity with the soil and loyalty.

Always gifted as an orator, Dostoyevsky swept the crowds off their feet with his proclamation of Pushkin's genius and his theory of Russia's Christian mission. He brought his wrath down on the heads of the westernizers. Russia, he stated, was not to be the lackey for European intellectualism. Any Russian who denies his affinity with the Russian soil betrays the Russian ideal. Only Russian beauty is pure and Pushkin was its greatest exponent.

The audience who listened to Dostoyevsky that night heard their country deified. Western Europe had become a conglomeration of atheist states and so would fall devastated before Russia. In his notes on the speech in the *Diary* Dostoyevsky said, 'Indeed, in the West there is no longer Christianity, there is no church, notwithstanding the fact that there still are many Christians who will never disappear, Catholicism, in truth, is no longer Christianity; gradually it is transforming itself into idolatry, while Protestantism with gigantic strides is being converted into atheism and into vacillating, fluent, variable (and not eternal) ethics.'[2]

Dostoyevsky's delivery was the best it had ever been. By the power of his oratory alone, he won his audience over. He described for Anna the effect of his speech on two listeners: 'Two old men, strangers to me, stopped me: "We have been enemies for twenty years, we have not spoken to one another, and now we have embraced and made peace. It is you who have reconciled us. You are our saint, you are our prophet!"'[3] Even Turgenev embraced him in tears. The reception was so rapturous that the crowd shouted, 'You are the prophet!' Dostoyevsky had to be taken bodily from the podium by his fellow writers. Women fainted at his feet and he was escorted through the wild crowds whose behaviour was more suited to a twentieth-century pop concert than a nineteenth-century literary gathering.

Dostoyevsky's triumph was short-lived. It was one thing to hear the speech delivered by a great orator with fire and passion to a large and enthusiastic crowd; it was quite another to read it in the cold light of day. Almost immediately the speech was denounced by Turgenev and other contemporary critics as romantic rubbish. Once again Dostoyevsky went from fame to ridicule in a short time, just as he had at the beginning of his career.

Nothing, however, could mar the triumph of *The Brothers Karamazov*. It sold out almost immediately and the Dostoyevskys began arranging a second edition as well as further editions of his other novels. Business was booming; Anna had now grasped the fundamentals of publishing and was to continue to build up Dostoyevsky's reputation for the rest of her life.

Dostoyevsky was now an established literary figure. He would not be able to fulfil his every literary dream, for he was never to write a life of Christ. But he had produced several masterpieces of which the world would be talking for the next hundred years and beyond. As *The Brothers Karamazov* went into print, however, Dostoyevsky knew that his own time was running out. His emphysema was untreatable now; the walls of his arteries and veins were like paper.

One night in January 1881 Dostoyevsky's sister, Vera, came to plead with him about their Aunt Kumamina's will, which they still disputed. As they talked about the issue, perhaps in heated debate, Dostoyevsky began to haemorrhage. Over the next few days his condition stabilized but it hovered between improvement and relapse until Dostoyevsky said to Anna, 'Today I am going to die.' She comforted him and told him he would not die but he insisted on the truth of it.

He asked her to get the New Testament that the wives of the Decembrists had given to him all those years ago. Like him, it had survived Siberia, misfortune and fame. She opened it and read, from where it fell open, the story of Christ's baptism by John. John tried to protest against the baptism because he felt unworthy but Jesus insisted that it go ahead: 'Let it be so now; for thus it is fitting for us to fulfil all righteousness.'[4]

Dostoyevsky, who often allowed himself to be guided by reading the Bible at random, saw great significance in this passage. He told Anna that the verse indicated that he was indeed going to die. Anna wrote: 'I could not restrain my tears. Fiodor began comforting me, saying kind and loving words and thanking me for the happy life he had enjoyed with me.'[5] Not long after the reading he fell into a coma and soon after that he died.

Throughout his life he had struggled with the knowledge of good and evil. He had tried to come to terms with the meaning of human free will in a world where God was the ultimate arbiter. He had advocated justice on earth for the poor. In his novels his characters wrestled with eternal questions and he portrayed the mechanism of doubt with genius. None of his characters possessed simple answers. As his life progressed, Dostoyevsky grew more courageous in proclaiming his own faith in God to his public but in his novels he could never shake off the darker side of human evil and doubt. Perhaps there was always a part of him that, like Shatov in *The Devils*, believed in Christ but in the end could only say 'I shall believe in God.'[6]

DOSTOYEVSKY

[1] Letter to Dr. A.F. Blagonravov, December 1880, *The Letters of Fyodor Michailovitch Dostoyevsky to his Family and Friends*, page 258.

[2] 'Concerning One Most Important Matter', *Diary of a Writer*, page 984.

[3] Letter to his wife, June 1880, *Dostoyevsky: Letters and Reminiscences*, pages 232–233.

[4] Matthew 3:15, Revised Standard Version.

[5] *Dostoevsky: Portrayed by his Wife — The Diary and Reminiscences of Mme. Dostoevsky*, page 187.

[6] *The Devils*, page 259.

4

4

BIBLIOGRAPHY
with acknowledgments

WORKS BY F. M. DOSTOYEVSKY

Poor Folk and *The Gambler*, tr. C. J. Hogarth. Everyman Classics, J. M. Dent & Sons Ltd, London 1987.

Notes from the Underground/The Double, tr. Jessie Coulson. Penguin Classics, Penguin Books Ltd, London 1988.

Notes from the Underground, White Nights, The Dream of a Ridiculous Man and Selections from The House of the Dead, tr. Andrew R. MacAndrew. Signet Classics, New English Library Limited, London 1961.

The House of the Dead, tr. H. Sutherland Edwards, Everyman Library, J. M. Dent & Sons Ltd, London 1979 (original edition 1911, revised 1962).

The Eternal Husband, tr. Constance Garnett. William Heinemann, London 1983.

The Village of Stepanchikovo, tr. Ignat Avsey. Classics, London 1983.

The Insulted and Injured, tr. Constance Garnett. William Heinemann, London 1915.

Crime and Punishment, tr. Constance Garnett. Pan Classics (in association with William Heinemann), London 1979.

The Idiot, tr. David Magarshack. Penguin Classics 1955. Quoted by permission of Penguin Books Ltd.

The Devils (The Possessed), tr. David Magarshack. Penguin Classics (Revised Edition) 1971. Quoted by permission of Penguin Books Ltd

A Raw Youth, tr. Constance Garnett. William Heinemann Ltd, London 1950.

The Brothers Karamazov (2 volumes), tr. David Magarshack. Penguin Classics 1958. Quoted by permission of Penguin Books Ltd.

The Crocodile, tr. S. C. Cioran. Ardis, Ann Arbor, Michigan 1988.

LETTERS AND JOURNALS OF F. M. DOSTOYEVSKY

The Letters of Fyodor Michailovitch Dostoyevsky to his Family and Friends, tr. Ethel Coburn Mayne. Peter Owen Publishers, London 1962. Quoted by permission.

Dostoevsky: Letters and Reminiscences, tr. S. S. Koteliansky and J. Middleton Murray. Chatto & Windus, London 1923.

Letters of Dostoevsky to His Wife, tr. Elizabeth Hill and Doris Mudie. Constable & Co. Ltd, London 1930.

Dostoyevsky: A Self Portrait, tr. Jessie Coulson. Oxford University Press, 1962. Quoted by permission of Oxford University Press.

Dostoevsky's Occasional Writings, tr. David Magarshack. Random House Inc., New York 1963. Random House Inc., New York 1963.

Summer Impressions, tr. with an introduction by Kyril Fitzlyon.

Notebooks for The Idiot, tr. Katherine Shelsky. The University of Chicago Press 1967.

Diary of a Writer (2 volumes), tr. Boris Brasol. Quotations from the *Diary* are reprinted by permission of Charles Scribner's Sons, an imprint of MacMillan Publishing Company, New York. Copyright 1949 Charles Scribner's Sons.

WORKS BY A. G. DOSTOYEVSKY

Dostoevsky: Portrayed by His Wife — The Diary and Reminiscences of Mme. Dostoevsky, tr. S. S. Koteliansky. George Routledge & Sons, Ltd, London 1926.

Dostoevsky, Reminiscences by Anna Dostoevsky, tr. Beatrice Stillman. Wildwood House, London 1976.

BIOGRAPHIES

Leonid Grossman, *Dostoevsky*. tr. Mary Mackler. Penguin Books Ltd, London 1974.

Geir Kjetsaa, *Fyodor Dostoyevsky: A Writer's Life*. tr. Siri Hustvedt and David McDuff. Macmillan, London 1988.

Joseph Frank, *Dostoevsky: Volume 1, The Seeds of Revolt, 1821-1849*. Princeton University Press. Princeton, New Yersey, 1976.

Joseph Frank, *Dostoevsky: Volume 2, The Years of Ordeal, 1850-1859*. Princeton University Press. Princeton, New Jersey, 1983.

Joseph Frank, *Dostoevsky: Volume 3, The Stir of Liberation, 1860-1865*. Princeton University Press. Princeton, New Jersey, 1986.

Ronald Hingley, *Dostoyevsky: His Life and Work*. Paul Elek, London. 1978.

David Magarshack, *Dostoevsky*. Secker & Warburg, London 1962.

OTHERS

A. Boyce Gibson, *The Religion of Dostoyevsky*. SCM Press Ltd, London 1973.

Ivan Dolenc, *Dostoevsky and Christ: A Study of Dostoyevsky's Rebellion Against Belinsky*. York Publishing & Printing Co., 1978.

John Jones, *Dostoevsky*. Oxford University Press, 1985.

F. M. Dostoevsky: Stavrogin's Confession, tr. Virginia Woolf and S. S. Koteliansky, with a Psychoanalytical Study of the Author by Sigmund Freud. Lear Publishers, New York 1947.

BIBLIOGRAPHY

Roger Anderson, *Dostoevsky: Myths of Duality*. University of Florida Press, 1986.

Charles E. Passage, *Character Names in Dostoevsky's Fiction*. Ardis, Ann Arbor, Michigan 1982.

Dostoevsky as Reformer: The Petrashevsky Case, ed. and tr. Liza Knapp. Ardis, An Arbor, Michigan 1987.

John Meyendorff, *The Orthodox Church*. St. Vladimir's Seminar Press, New York 1981.

Richard Pipes, *Russia Under the Old Regime*. Penguin Books, 1987.

Hugh Seton-Watson, *The Russian Empire 1801-1917. Oxford Modern History of Europe*. Oxford University Press, 1988.

Richard Deacon, *A History of the Russian Secret Service*. Grafton Books, Collins, London 1987.

INDEX

Alekseyevsky Ravelin 39, 41, 45
Alexander I (Tsar) 54
Alexander II (Tsar) 76, 81
anti-hero characterization 91, 106-07,
  157 *see also* 'underground man'
Antonelli, Pyotr 38

Bad Ems spa, Germany 141
Bakunin, Mikhail 116, 128
  Revolutionary Catechism 128
Balzac, *Eugénie Grandet* 23
Beketov circle 33-34
Belinsky, Vissarion 27-31, 32-33, 37,
  42-43, 44, 143, 151, 161
Bible 44, 55, 92, 131, 167
Blagonravov, A.F. 163
Borodino, battle of 7
Brown, Martha 98
Bulgarian rebellion (1876) 148, 151

Chernyshevsky 83
Citizen, The (newspaper) 138-40
Coleridge 79
Constantinople 149-50, 152
Contemporary, The (magazine) 33,
  84-85, 94

Danilevsky, Nikolai *Russia and Europe*
  124
Danilov, Foma 151
Darovoye 12-14, 21-22
Dawn (magazine) 124

Decembrists (rebellion) 17, 54-55
  wives 54-56, 167
Dickens, Charles 66, 147, 154
Dostoyevskaya, Anna (née Snitkina)
  100-04, 110-13, 132, 135-40, 163-67
Dostoyevskaya, Maria Dmitryevna
  73-77, 79, 85, 88-93, 96, 98, 104,
  147
Dostoyevskaya, Maria Fyodorovna
  Nechayeva 8, 10, 13-14
Dostoyevskaya, Sofia 137
Dostoyevskaya, Sonya 116
Dostoyevskaya, Vera 137, 167
Dostoyevsky, Andrei 14, 21, 41-42
Dostoyevsky, Fyodor Mikhailovich
  life — (chronological)
  childhood 8-14
  military career 15-22, 24-25
  early literary career 23-34
  Ravelin 38-45
  trial and mock execution 45-48
  Siberia 48-65
  marriage to Maria 77, 85
  return to Petersburg 79, 81-84
  first tour of Europe 85
  tour of Europe with Polina 86-88
  marriage to Anna 97, 101-04
  third tour of Europe 111-26
  birth of children 116, 126, 136
  return to Russia 135ff
  two-day gaol sentence 139-40
  spa at Bad Ems 141

INDEX

last years 163-67

life (cont)
anti-Semitism 154-56
aural hallucinations 13, 25, 36
epilepsy 32, 36-37, 56, 77-79, 104,
  113, 136, 140
gambling 87, 112, 116, 122
nationalism 84, 114, 123-25, 149,
  154, 163, 165
religious identity 20, 29-30,
  33-34, 44-45, 57, 63, 68-69, 71,
  95, 106, 108, 133, 136-37, 142,
  152, 159-63, 167
socialist ideas 61-63, 144, 150
spiritualism 147-48
xenophobia 85, 114, 123
works — (chronological)
Poor Folk (1846) 9, 26-28, 74, 140,
  143
The Double (1846) 20, 30, 33, 91,
  140
Uncle's Dream (1859) 77
The House of the Dead (1861-62)
  58-60, 63, 75, 86
The Village of Sepanchikovo
  (1861-62) 77
Notes from Underground (1864)
  89-91, 93, 96
Crime and Punishment (1866) 15, 64,
  73, 90-93, 95, 101, 104-08, 110,
  119, 133, 139, 145
The Gambler (1866) 101
The Idiot (1868-69) 78, 87, 95, 115,
  117-21, 137, 139, 157
The Devils (The Possessed)
  (1871-72) 90-93, 106, 117, 123,
  128-33, 137-39, 145, 156, 167
A Raw Youth 140
Diary of a Writer (1876-81) 16, 63,
  140, 142-46, 148, 154, 159, 165
The Brothers Karamazov
  (1879-80) 22, 60, 68, 90, 92-95,
  142, 148, 156-63, 166

'The Grand Inquisitor' 160-62;
  (unpublished) *Atheism* 95, 122-23
The Life of a Great Sinner 91, 123
  (periodicals) *see Time, Epoch, The
  Citizen*
Dostoyevsky, Fyodor (Fedya) 136,
  138
Dostoyevsky, Lyubov 22, 126
Dostoyevsky, Dr Mikhail
  Andreyevich 7-13, 15, 19, 21-22
Dostoyevsky, Mikhail (brother of
  Fyodor) 8, 12, 14-15, 17-18, 20, 24,
  26, 40-42, 49-51, 54, 65-66, 70, 79,
  83, 86, 93, 96-98, 110
Durov 46, 49-50, 53-54, 56, 61, 67, 84
Durov circle 35-37, 42, 54

Epoch (magazine) 93-94, 96-98, 124

Fedorovna, Emilia 51
feudal system 28-29 *see also* serfs
Feuerbach, *The Essence of Christianity*
  29, 34
Fillipov, Danilo 130
Fonvizina, Natalya 55-56, 68, 132
Fourier/ism 28-29, 33-34, 37, 62, 124
Freud, Sigmund 22, 37, 77, 156
Frolovna, Alyona (nurse) 10, 14, 21
Fyodorovna, Katerina 154

Garibaldi, 116
Geneva, international peace
  conference 116
Gogol, Nikolai Vasilievich 37, 42-43
  The Inspector General 84
Grigorovich, Dmitry 26-27, 30, 37, 77
Grigoryev, Nikolay 47

Hegel 29, 128
Herzen 87
Holbein the Younger, *The Dead Christ
  in the Tomb* 115-16
Hugo, Victor 19, 163 *The Last Day of a
  Condemned Man* 49

INDEX

Ilyinsky (Prince) 60, 157
Isayev, Alexander 73-75
Isayeva, Maria, *see* Dostoyevskaya
Isayev, Pasha 73, 79, 89, 97, 110-11,
 121-22, 136
Islam 53-65, 151
Ivanov, Ivan 127-29

Jastrzenbski 53-54

Kant, *Critique of Reason* 66
Katkov 107, 121, 137, 140
Kiev 10
Kjetsaa, Geir 131
Koran 66
Kornilova, Yekaterina 145
Krayevsky 33, 51
Krivtsov (Major) 56, 78
Krukovskaya, Anna Korvin 98-100,
 103
Krukovskaya, Sophia 99-100
Kumamin, Alexander 8, 22, 25
Kumamina, (Aunt) 8-9, 18, 22, 25, 137
Kuznetsk 75, 76

Lebedov 43
Liprandi 43-44
London 85, 125

Maikov, Apollon 33, 36, 40-41, 43,
 113, 116-17, 121, 124-25
Maikov, Valerian 33-34
Marey (peasant) 13, 64
Mariinsky Hospital for the Poor 7-8,
 11-12
Meshchersky (Prince) 138-39
Military Academy for Engineers 14, 67
Milyukov 49-50, 101, 107
Moscow 7, 8, 10, 164-65

Nechayev, Sergei 128-29
Nekrasov, Nicolai 26-27, 30, 33,
 84-85, 94-95, 139-40, 164
Nicholas I, (Tsar) 17, 19, 35, 39,
 42-43, 45, 54-55, 76
Nicholas II (Tsar) 82, 139, 142
Notes of the Fatherland 33, 140

Orthodox Christianity, *see* Russian
 Orthodox church
Osmidov, N. L. 105

Panayev, Avdotya 74
Panayev, Ivan 74
Pan-Slavic movement 149
papacy 150, 152
Paris Commune 99-100, 150
Pavlovna, Elena 100-01
Petrashevsky circle 34-40, 45-47, 54,
 59, 116
Petrashevsky, Mikhail 34-35, 43, 46,
 48-49, 53, 67
phalansteries 28-29, 43, 62
plebeian intelligentsia 27
Poland, 1863 rebellion 85
Polina, *see* Suslova, Apollinaria
Protestantism 150-51, 166
Pushkin, Aleksander Sergeevich 14,
 19, 154, 164-65

Riesenkampf (Dr) 24-25
Roman Catholicism 7, 119, 125,
 150-51, 161, 166
Rostovsky, St Dmitry 44
Russia,
 nobility 9
 Christianity 10
 Asian 52-53
 emancipation of serfs 81
 westernizers 114, 165
 war with Turkey 149-52
Russian Orthodox church 7, 11, 12,
 29, 37, 38, 42, 45, 65, 95, 106, 119,
 122-24, 147, 149, 151-52, 155, 161
Russification 85-86
Russophiles 124-25

St Peter and Paul fortress 38-39, 77,
 129

INDEX

St Petersburg 15-18, 22, 26, 50-51, 79,
    81, 85
    1862 fires 82-83
    Trinity Cathedral 104
    poverty 104
St Sergey, Trinity Monastery of 11
Salvador 86-87
Sand, George 19
Schiller, *The Robbers* 9
Scott, Walter 19, 154
Semipalatinsk 65-67, 70-71, 87
Semyonovsky Square 45-46, 70
serfs 12-13, 21-22, 28-29, 35, 81-83,
    144
Sheransky, Anatoly (Nathan) 59
Shidlovsky 20-21
Siberia 21-22, 40-41
Slavophiles 123-25
Snitkin, Ivan 128
Solzhenitsyn, Alexander 59
Speshnev, Nikolai 35, 37, 40, 47
Stellovsky 101, 103
Strakhov, Nikolai 85-86, 113, 124, 132
Strauss, David 34
Sumarokov, Adjutant General 47
Sunday school movement 84

Suslova, Apollinaria (Polina) 86-88
Swedenborg 147

Time (magazine) 83-86, 93, 94, 124,
    135
Tolstoy, Leo 132
    Anna Karenina 140
Totlebon, Adolph 24
Totlebon, Eduard (General) 24, 76-77,
    79
Turgenev, Ivan 30, 84-85, 94-95,
    114-15, 154, 163, 165
    Fathers and Sons 107
Tver 79

'underground man' characterization
    89-93
Uniate church 7

Wrangel Alexander (Baron) 69-71,
    73-77, 87, 96-97

Yanovsky, Stepan 32, 36, 40, 57

Zschokke, H. D. 20, 28

A selection of biographies from LION PUBLISHING

C. S. LEWIS William Griffin	£6.95	☐
GEORGE MACDONALD William Raeper	£5.95	☐
HANNAH MORE Margaret and Jeremy Collingwood	£4.99	☐
HERE I STAND Roland H. Bainton	£5.99	☐
THE JOURNAL OF JOHN WESLEY Christopher Idle	£5.95	☐
JOHN CALVIN T.H.L. Parker	£5.95	☐
GEORGE WHITEFIELD AND THE GREAT AWAKENING John Pollock	£5.95	☐
WILBERFORCE John Pollock	£5.95	☐
SHAFTESBURY John Pollock	£5.99	☐

All Lion paperbacks are available from your local bookshop or newsagent, or can be ordered direct from the address below. Just tick the titles you want and fill in the form.

Name (Block Letters) _____

Address _____

_____

_____

Write to Lion Publishing, Cash Sales Department, PO Box 11, Falmouth, Cornwall TR10 9EN, England.

Please enclose a cheque or postal order to the value of the cover price plus:

UK: 80p for the first book, 20p for each additional book ordered to a maximum charge of £2.00.

OVERSEAS INCLUDING EIRE: £1.50 for the first book, £1.00 for the second book and 30p for each additional book.

BFPO: 80p for the first book, 20p for each additional book.

Lion Publishing reserves the right to show on covers and charge new retail prices which may differ from those previously advertised in the text or elsewhere, and to increase postal rates in accordance with the Post Office.